Explaining AI

An Overview of Artificial Intelligence Concepts

LJ Bubb

In the beginning there was a BBC micro. Thanks folks.

Table of Contents

Introduction

Artificial Intelligence (AI) and Machine Learning (ML) have come to particular prominence in recent years with a sudden surge of interest and investment in the technologies. The two terms are often used interchangeably in general parlance and no great distinction is made in this book, although academics and practitioners can prefer to apply somewhat more nuanced definitions that draw a distinction.

There are many tasks that are easy for a human to perform but are relatively difficult for a machine (and also vice versa). This observation is known as Moravec's paradox and contrasts the apparent difficulty of implementing human-like cognitive abilities (such as common sense reasoning and perception) in computers with the relative ease of programming tasks that require logical and analytical processing.

AI is the general subject area of trying to persuade a machine to perform tasks that have traditionally been difficult to automate but a human is capable of performing.

Machine learning is the more specific idea of enabling a machine to comprehend data without requiring specially programmed rules. Machine learning is a very significant component of AI and a frequently used tool but it is sometimes possible to implement AI by other methods. AI is more of a broad umbrella term referring to a wide field of study of which machine learning is a subset.

Software is written as an intricate sequence of instructions that are followed precisely. A computer is told every action that must be performed and precisely how it must achieve the task. Programming a computer is like an extreme form of micro-management. The computer has to be instructed at an incredibly detailed and low level of granularity as to how each step must be accomplished.

When text is displayed in a window on a screen the system must be informed which characters are to be drawn and the exact position of each character on the screen. The system must be told the appropriate spacing between the characters and the correct distance between the lines of text.

The system must be told what pattern of pixels comprises each character, usually as a sequence of shapes that must be drawn which enables the characters to be more easily scaled to any size. The machine is told a "Z" is composed of two straight parallel lines of even length that are connected by one diagonal line and the lines are to be one pixel wide. The lines are defined by points at either end that are separated in a particular ratio. The machine must be told exactly how a straight line is to be drawn between two points. Someone programmed in the rules for diacritics to render foreign languages, such as which characters in French have an acute accent and exactly how the accent is combined with the character.

The characters are "anti-aliased" or blended with the background. The characters fade out at the edges in shades of grey to avoid sharp contrasts that are not aesthetically appealing. Someone programmed specifically how this was to be done and exactly which shade of grey to use in which situation to produce an artistic effect. Someone told the machine how to redraw the characters when bold type variations are applied or the look of the characters when they are italicised.

When characters reach close to the edge of a window, someone determined the rules for when words wrap onto the next line. The computer should look back to the previous space and move the entire word as one unit rather than just breaking the word part way through. The system needs to handle exceptions for hyphens or what happens if the word is part of a quotation and starts with a quote mark, in which case the punctuation needs to be moved as well. When quotes are used, is it an open quote or a close quote that is being typed? It is the same key on the keyboard for both but many fonts use a different character style for each quote mark depending on the context. Someone added rules to handle that.

When a window is moved, it might overlap another. Only part of the text that is not overlapped must be displayed. This all has to be calculated and rules programmed. When a window reaches the edge of the screen, the part that is beyond the edge is obscured. That is, unless the user has multiple monitors in which case the system must calculate which screen the part of the window might appear on. The window needs to then be split in two with half displayed on one screen and half on another. The other monitor might be a different resolution and a portion of the window may need to be scaled.

The instructions the programmer types are usually not really the instructions that are executed by the hardware. The programmer is working at a high level of abstraction and all of the instructions from the programmer are converted into "machine code" that the computer actually interprets. This machine readable code works at a very low level of granularity indeed. Language at this level might only be capable of informing the computer to place a number in a specific location in memory, then fetching the number, performing some computations on that value and returning it to a different location in memory. Programming within the highly restrictive constraints of this simple language is far too cumbersome for day-to-day use and most programmers don't write at this level. A translator (compiler) is used to convert from a higher-level form that is much more flexible and easier to write. Again a programmer defined in detail how this translation was to be done.

When the image is finally calculated it is not in a form that is suited to the monitor. Someone programmed (or maybe a hardware engineer produced equivalent circuits) to determine how the image would be converted into a series of electrical pulses that the monitor input interface understands.

At the beginning of personal computers, software engineers often had to handle all of these complications themselves and understand everything about the machine they were programming in detail right down to the way the image was represented on the screen. In more recent times a programmer is rarely expected to deal directly with the great majority of these considerations. They may define some text and say which window it is to be displayed in and that's the end of the matter from their perspective. The reason this is now so much easier is the wide availability of software libraries of pre-written code.

Software libraries are packages of software that handle all of the low-level complications of dealing with the machine. Basic packages for handling matters such as the display of text and drawing windows are now included as standard with an operating system. An operating system is in fact just a standardised bundle of packages of software to assist the programmer. However, this doesn't avoid the fact that somewhere a programmer has been required to write all of the instructions down at a ridiculously minute level of detail. It is just that in modern times a coder is almost always able to buy in (or find for free) ready-written instructions from another programmer and simply copy them, which makes the task of displaying text tremendously easier.

Writing lists of instructions is not always feasible though. For some tasks it's very difficult indeed. Handwriting recognition is a notoriously difficult task to program a sequence of instructions to accomplish. That is, given a scan or photo of a document, identify what has been written. Perhaps a postal service would like to have a machine recognise handwritten addresses on an envelope so that an automated sorting robot knows where to deliver them.

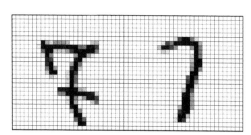

Figure 1 - Two different samples of handwritten "7' digits

A programmer might initially attempt to approach this problem by taking an example of a handwritten character and then comparing all of the pixels in an example to the scan presented from the envelope. The problem is that no two images of the same handwritten character look exactly alike (see Figure 1).

Sometimes the handwriting styles are quite distinct. Sometimes the character is written slightly slanted one way or another or slightly rotated. Sometimes it is larger or smaller. It may have been written on different colours and shades of paper using pens with different thicknesses and weights. Part of the character may be missing. It may be joined writing or printed writing. There may be accidental ink blots or marks on the page that need to be ignored. What if the handwriting is crossed out?

The programmer needs to consider which specific pixels in the scan contribute to each character and write rules for every pattern of pixels that may appear. There are so many variations it is exceptionally difficult to manually program all of the combinations that may come up. Programming the rules is not impossible, it's just very time consuming. There will always be one more exception that has not been thought about. Writing a program to perform the jobs AI is performing is always theoretically possible, but may involve such a huge amount of labour that it is impractically expensive and time consuming. If you need to employ all the programmers that exist for a hundred years, the job may as well be impossible.

A machine learning system presents a much more convenient and considerably faster alternative to writing a vast list of rules. It avoids the necessity to program the machine at all. The machine is instead presented with large numbers of examples of what handwritten characters look like and effectively programs itself from the set of examples to do the job of interpreting the characters.

Part of the problem may still be programmed by a human, such as identifying the location of the writing on the envelope and the code necessary to operate the scanning machine. However, the most challenging part of the programming problem is passed to the machine learning system.

Examples of other tasks that are very difficult to directly program and easier to tackle with a machine learning approach include:

- Speech recognition - taking an audio file and transcribing what was said into text
- Recognising objects in images e.g. detecting a person in a video feed
- Assisting robots in navigating around using sensors e.g. self driving cars
- Pattern analysis in data such as finding trends in financial information for investment purposes or fraud detection.
- Medical diagnosis: given the medical history of a patient and a set of test results, what condition might they have?
- Optimisation: finding the best method of approaching a task from many alternatives

- Natural language (human language) manipulation tasks e.g. translating between different languages or understanding the intent of what has been asked of the machine by a person

The skills of the human programmer and the machine learning system are usually blended together with parts of the problems being tackled by whichever approach is most appropriate and then the parts are combined into a complete system. Training a machine learning system by example can be cumbersome and hard work. The outcome from the learning process is not always what the programmer intended or the machine fails to learn at all and a great deal of work is necessary to persuade it to learn. Machine learning is not a panacea that replaces all programming.

It would be a waste of time to train a machine learning system to add up a column of numbers when it can be so trivially directly informed to do so with traditional software. Machine learning is more of a useful tool to slot into a programmer's arsenal for attacking specific difficult problems rather than a generalised Swiss army knife that is the answer to everything. However, there are many problems that are so fiendishly difficult to program, machine learning is a much better alternative.

There are now machine learning systems that can themselves write conventional software (as a set of instructions) and use of these systems has exploded.

However, they are usually only appropriate for delivering short sections of code to the specification of a programmer. The capability of the current generation of AI tools to coherently produce longer pieces of code is very limited. Demonstrations of AI systems apparently writing completed software can be found, but these come with significant caveats and are somewhat misleading.

Programmers have always used reference material and have looked up standard solutions to problems, first in books and later on the web. The machine that can write code is the latest incarnation of the programmer's reference book. It has all the answers immediately available and can cleverly customise the answers it has found to more closely fit the problem which saves a lot of time. What these tools can't do, at least today, is reliably write a complex system from start to finish to the specification of a user untrained in the art of software development. What they can do is deliver a helpful toolbox of pre-written components very quickly, like software libraries, to a human programmer to help accelerate software delivery.

A lot of the programmer's job is figuring out what the customer actually wants. What does it mean when the marketing department wants to strategise for the cloud age? The problem rarely comes with the kind of clear and precise specification that an AI coding system can feasibly follow. The marketing department doesn't want to write a twenty page, tightly worded formal specification for the format data will arrive in and another twenty page specification for the format data will be delivered in. They want someone else to make it happen for them.

The programmer of today is a designer and an orchestrator, wrangling software libraries into what it is imagined is required and then making iterative corrections. Perhaps tomorrow the programmer is wrangling AI written software as well, working out how best to glue these components together into what the customer actually asked for and filling in the gaps for the parts that the AI cannot deliver.

When new software generation tools appear, the programmer doesn't vanish, they just move to a higher level of abstraction in the code production process. Most people in the world don't enjoy figuring out how to make all of these complex tools work together and don't want to know anything about bits and bytes. They just want it to work. The programmer will continue to find employment even in the age of machines that can code, probably even more employment, with the near unlimited demand for automation and the new applications that are unlocked by AI techniques.

The rise of AI driven systems has the potential to change the shape of many industries with jobs being eliminated and new jobs being created. We may soon be in a position where it is feasible for a product to be transported from the factory gates to your home with little or no human intervention. The transport industry may see the advent of self-driving vehicles slowly but surely replacing human drivers. Container ships can now be loaded and unloaded by robots. Warehouse robots are transporting goods back and forth from shelves.

The creative industries might be disrupted by generative AI. There are machines that can produce art and realistic photographs. There are machines that can assist with the production of music and help with creative writing.

Massive customer service call centres might be disrupted by AI chatbots. Whether customers like speaking to the AI or not, they may be given little choice by companies looking to cut costs.

AI driven robots might replace people in the fast food industry. There are already robots that can prepare meals. The job of a cashier in the fast food chains has been displaced by display screens that take orders. Robots might replace people in agriculture, leaving few low skilled jobs to be done. Machines are now available that can pick fruits. Robots can now eliminate weeds. It is only a matter of time until the cost of the robots can undercut the wages of seasonal labour. Many of these jobs may disappear.

We're currently at the beginning of an AI renaissance, witnessing the dawn of a transformative era that holds the promise of reshaping many aspects of our lives. Industries are about to be disrupted.

How Machine Learning Works

Say we want to persuade a machine to tell the difference between elephants and mice, a problem called "classification". The first thing that needs to be done is to determine some factors that might reliably differentiate one animal from the other. Perhaps the heights and weights of the animals may be chosen. These are factors that can be easily measured and sound in theory as if they might result in metrics that are quite distinct for each type of animal. It would be anticipated that the heights and weights of elephants and mice are quite different.

We don't have to choose only height and weight. As many factors as we like can be collected. You can use your intuition about which factors could be relevant to the task and the assumptions do not necessarily need to be correct. If you went with the number of eyes and it turns out elephants and mice both have exactly two eyes, it doesn't matter as our machine learning system will automatically figure out that number of eyes isn't a very useful way of telling the animals apart. You will need to have guessed some factors that are relevant to the task somewhere in the mix, but you don't need to know exactly which factors are important.

We might start our quest for AI with a brainstorming session, asking people who are experts in the field to use their experience to throw out ideas regarding which factors might be significant. The next thing we need to do is collect some "training" examples for the system to learn from. That is, real world measurements of elephants and mice are taken and the heights and weights are recorded in a table.

Height (cm)	Weight (kg)	Animal
330	4937	Elephant
4.5	0.031	Mouse
310	4276	Elephant
4.1	0.026	Mouse
...	...	...

In this specific trivial example we're not going to need a great deal of training data. Normally you need to be able to acquire "a lot" of training examples. The quotes are there because a lot is not well defined. There's no magic number of examples, it might be ten examples or it might be a million that are necessary.

There is research into trying to persuade machines to learn with only a small number of examples. It must be possible because kids do it. You take your toddler to the farm and point them at a cow, a sheep and a pig. Next time you take them back they know which one is which or maybe you need to correct them once or twice. However you didn't need to take them 50,000 times and show them a moo moo from every possible angle and under every lighting condition. However, with your regular machine learning system as it stands at the moment, a single example is going to be insufficient. A significant caveat should be applied to that statement because learning from only a few examples is an ongoing area of investigation and the technology might change very soon in some areas. We know it's definitely possible to get it to work due to the evidence that humans are capable of performing the task. It's just a matter of time before the machines catch up.

OK, so let's put our data on a chart (see Figure 2).

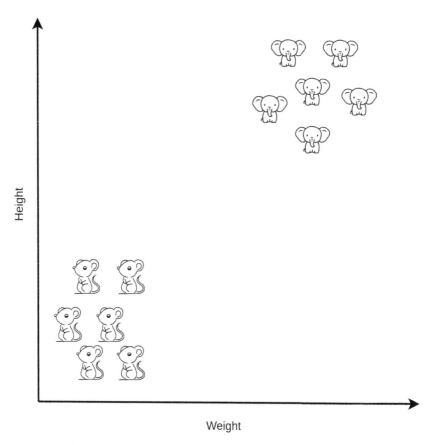

Figure 2 - Height versus weight data for elephants and mice plotted on a chart

We can clearly see that elephants tend to be in the upper right of the chart and mice tend to be in the lower left of the chart. This is not surprising as elephants tend to be large and heavy and mice tend to be small and light.

We could draw an imaginary line dividing the two distinct regions of the chart (see Figure 3). What if I gave you some new measurements, but didn't tell you what kind of animal they came from? The new example is very heavy and big. If I asked you to place that unknown animal on the chart it would end up near the top right.

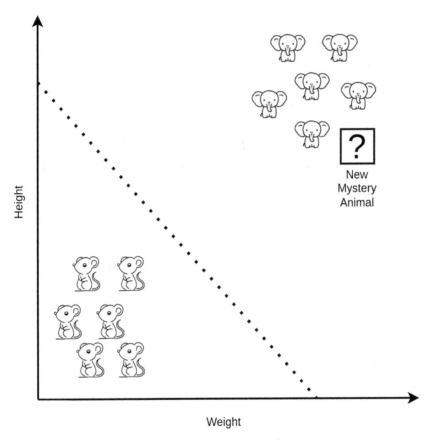

Figure 3 - A dividing line is drawn between the two separate categories. A new unknown animal is added to the chart.

Given what else is around it in that region of the chart, we're going to conclude it's most likely an elephant. What we just did there is called "inference" and AI can do that for us. Instead of needing to manually inspect the chart, a machine can examine the nearby examples and draw a conclusion as to which group the new example is most similar to. That's quite a useful capability as if we had a million sets of measurements we needed to classify as elephant or mouse, the machine can do the job for us in seconds whereas it would take forever by hand.

The way the machine is working is roughly what you did in your head. It draws a line on the chart and if the measurement is to the right of the line, it's an elephant and if the measurement is to the left of the line it's a mouse. "Machine learning" is the process of getting the computer to automatically decide where to draw the line on the chart by itself, without human involvement. In AI parlance, the dividing line that results from machine learning is known as a "model" as it represents or models the data.

The dividing line doesn't have to be a straight line either, there are different classes of machine learning algorithms. I've listed those main classes here using the genuine formal mathematical nomenclature:

- Ones that draw straight lines (as in Figure 3)
- Ones that draw wavy lines (as in Figure 4)
- Ones that lasso a bit of the chart (as in Figure 5)

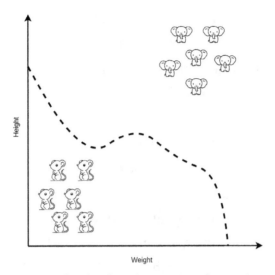

Figure 4 - Wavy line (nonlinear) separation of categories

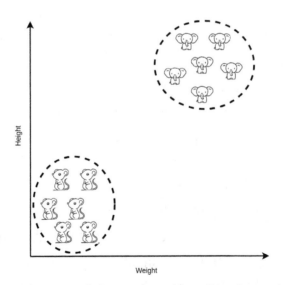

Figure 5 - Lasso style (nonparametric) bounding of categories

The machine learning system that can draw a wavy line (or estimates a nonlinear function is perhaps how a mathematician may put it) seems more capable than the one that can only draw straight lines. The elephants and mice may not appear on the chart such that a straight line can easily go between them. A curved line can go around corners and bend into a more complex shape that can weave and thread between awkward data points. Being able to lasso a section of the chart seems as if it should be even more capable still. However, it's not so straightforward to decide that any one of these techniques is necessarily better than another. Firstly, there are often clever mathematical ways of avoiding the problem. The data may be rearranged such that the apparently less capable straight line drawer can actually solve the problem when it seems only a wavy line will do the job. Secondly, the different types of separation have differing costs and benefits.

One reason why we might want to use one method over another is inference performance. If you expect to need to test a million data items per day but your inference takes even a second for a computer to process, that could be an issue as there are only 86,400 seconds in a day and you would never be able to get through the million data items. The lasso algorithm (or "nonparametric" might be the maths description) may seem initially attractive but the straight line drawer is actually vastly faster when you have a lot of inference to do. The counterpoint though is the reliability of the response of the algorithm to the problem. The lasso style method can give better quality answers when there is not much training data available, which might be preferred in some situations even though the performance is slower. So there are swings and roundabouts to consider, it's not just a simple case of one machine learning algorithm being obviously superior to any other.

As well as these broad classes of machine learning there are different subtypes within the classes. Deciding which one is optimal is a black art. Sometimes choices can be driven by the kinds of inputs the machine learning algorithm accepts or what kinds of output it can produce. For example some algorithms only really deal with binary true/false inputs, some deal with continuous numbers and some with selections from a list (labels). However, there's usually some clever way to bend the inputs you have into what an algorithm can accept. You can often get any data into any algorithm somehow with enough thought.

For example, say you have a machine learning algorithm that can only accept true or false binary inputs, but your data contains categories like "elephant" and "mouse", what can be done is turn each category into a binary choice. Is it an elephant? True or false. Is it a mouse? True or false. Is it a squirrel? True or false, etc. So the way the data is presented can be modified to fit the algorithm.

Some algorithms don't like missing values. For example, say you were able to measure a specific elephant's height but it was giving trouble when you tried to measure its weight and it stormed off. With some algorithms you can feed in just the height without the weight and it can still use the training data item provided there are at least some other examples where the weight is present. Other algorithms can't handle that situation which makes the algorithm useless where there is only patchy training data. Some algorithms are more resilient to errors in the data (noise) but others are not very tolerant of errors at all, preferring clean and accurate training data. If you have one person on your elephant measuring team who does not know how to use a tape measure, that could be a problem as there will be mistakes in the data.

Sometimes the algorithm choice might be based on the outputs. A system may only be able to make a single decision (it's an elephant or a mouse and never both) but other algorithms may permit the output to have more than one category. The data looks mostly like an elephant but there is always the outside possibility it could be a mouse, I'll give you a 95% probability it's an elephant and a 5% chance it's a mouse. The algorithm might be able to handle hierarchies of sub-categories, for example it's an elephant, but within that category it's an African elephant.

Then there's the computational performance of training. The AI probably isn't going to learn flawlessly the first time, in fact it may not even work at all. So you're going to want to iterate through many experiments. It's not uncommon for training on complex tasks with a lot of training data to take several days even on a very expensive and powerful machine. This is particularly so with video, image and audio tasks. If you have to wait several days between each iteration of your experiment, that really slows you down. If you imagine writing a computer program and each time you want to test the software it takes three days to get the error messages back, that's going to make progress exceptionally slow going. An AI software developer is going to be able to work much more efficiently (and hence solve the business problem faster) with a well selected algorithm that trains quickly so they can iterate through all of the problems faster.

All of this AI stuff looks fairly simple, you just put the data on a chart and draw a line and that's it. Why would you even need a machine at all? Well in this simple example you don't, you can just look at the chart, the solution is obvious and you can program in a rule by hand. When machine learning becomes particularly useful is where it's difficult for a human to see the answer to a problem.

The above chart has only two dimensions (height and weight) and two possible categories of animal to decide between. But with some problems we're going to need many more dimensions. What if we added a third dimension? So maybe we're going to add ear size as a third parameter to be measured to separate elephants and mice on the chart. This can still be visualised on a chart, just about, but now a dividing line has to be drawn in 3D space, which is tricky.

But what if we add length of tail. Now we're up to four dimensional space. How do you represent four dimensions on a chart? So we have the X-axis, the Y-axis, the Z-axis and ... ? Is that a hypercube? Perhaps it is something to do with a tesseract? How is a dividing line to be drawn now (see Figure 6)?

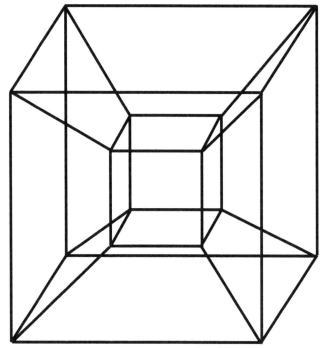

Figure 6 - A tesseract

What about five dimensions? I have absolutely no idea how to draw a five dimensional chart so we're going to need some help. This is where the machine learning comes in because unlike humans it can draw the dividing line in fairly well any number of dimensions. The fact that the machine can deal with very large numbers of dimensions allows us to do things that we would have a very difficult time figuring out on our own.

A task where the number of dimensions really starts increasing precipitously is when dealing with image data. Say we want to categorise pictures of elephants or mice instead of labelling them by measured characteristics. We go out and get our training data, that is thousands upon thousands of photos of elephants and mice, but how do you feed those pictures into a machine learning algorithm?

Imagine a greyscale photograph of 1000x1000 pixels. Traditionally the brightness of each pixel would be represented as a number between 0 and 255 because each pixel usually occupies one byte of memory, which can represent only that specific range of numbers. The 0 - 255 range of brightness values is usually sufficient to fool the human eye into thinking it is observing a continuous range of greys and is also a convenient range of numbers for a machine to work with.

Each pixel could be imagined as representing a dimension on a chart. The first pixel we encounter becomes the X-axis on the chart, the second pixel is the Y-axis, the third pixel is the Z-axis and so on up. With a 1000x1000 pixel image, then one million dimensions will be needed.

The data is not really conceptually much different to the chart of heights and weights, it's just got considerably more dimensions. A million dimensions is well beyond the capability of a human to work out how to draw a dividing line. However, a machine learning algorithm can achieve this. One dimension or a million dimensions is all the same to a computer. The only issue with a large number of dimensions is how much computing power is required for the system to learn (draw the dividing line) and that is a problem that can get out of hand. With a million dimensions, many calculations needed per dimension and perhaps a 100,000 items of training data, the requirements for machine learning might stretch the capability of the available computer. A machine can certainly be easily found that can tackle a task of this magnitude but machine learning becomes either slow or expensive (take your pick). There are, however, methods of improving the situation.

Audio data can be considered just a series of dimensions as well. You may have seen an oscillogram or waveform representation of an audio signal (see Figure 7):

Figure 7 - Oscillogram representation of an audio signal

The Y-axis of the oscillogram is the amplitude of the audio signal, which is a representation of the position of the speaker cone. This can move in one dimension, either backwards or forwards. The X-axis represents time. The waveform is broken down into samples. Often 44,100 samples per second is considered the magic number for acceptable audio fidelity for music, hence there are this number of positions along the X-axis per second of audio. There are also a distinct number of steps in amplitude, usually 65,536 is considered acceptable to produce reasonable audio quality. Hence, there are this number of possible distinct positions for the speaker cone.

In an audio signal, the first sample could be the first dimension on the machine learning chart, the 2nd sample the 2nd dimension and so on. It quickly becomes apparent though that this is going to result in a lot of dimensions for any reasonable length of audio. A typical three minute song would be nearly 8 million dimensions, and that's only in mono. Often it will be the case that some trick is applied to reduce the number of dimensions before machine learning is attempted. The audio will likely be mathematically simplified before presentation to a machine learning system.

If the intent is to recognise the genre of a song, aspects of the beat or melody may be examined as opposed to the complete waveform of the music. That might be good enough to do the job. The beat of a piece of audio can be easily extracted with conventional mathematical techniques and no machine learning is needed. Beat detectors are often available even on quite simple audio equipment. If the time between beats is presented as the input, there are perhaps two beats per second in a typical song and in a three minute song there are now only 360 items of information (beat timings) to be dealt with instead of 8 million items.

The process of extracting just what we need from the original data is called "feature extraction" and can massively reduce the number of dimensions down to a manageable level. Feature extractors are common where there is complex input data that might result in a lot of dimensions. Feature extractors on images might perform edge detection, which looks for sharp contrasts. An edge detector is a commonly seen image effect that produces an output from a photograph that looks somewhat like a cartoon.

Another useful process to help reduce computation is dimensionality reduction. This attempts to reduce the number of dimensions whilst still retaining most of the original meaning in the data. A simple way to think about this is scaling down an image, which reduces the number of pixels in it and therefore the number of dimensions that need to be input to the machine learning system. In fact, scaling down an image is a common preprocessing step to reduce the cost of machine learning. The image is still recognisable even at a size significantly smaller than the original.

There are statistical methods that can work on many forms of data and effectively try and scale down the number of dimensions in the data sets whilst still ensuring that what the data set represents still resembles (in a mathematical sense) the original data. One common technique is called "principal component analysis." With fewer dimensions it can be much quicker to perform machine learning.

Computer hardware is getting faster and faster and what is easily possible now would have been an incredible feat only a few years ago. Machine learning can increasingly just deal with very complex data sets up-front without requiring much pre-work and figure out the whole thing itself. However, the tasks researchers are going to want to attempt will always push the boundaries of what affordable hardware can do. There is always more data with greater fidelity and ever larger numbers of dimensions. Equally the consumer is going to hope to run sophisticated AI techniques on exceptionally cheap throw-away hardware with minimal computational capability. First the consumer expected a £20 doorbell to contain a wireless camera. Now the consumer wants the £20 camera to automatically detect an approaching courier so they never miss a delivery (how they get the courier detecting camera delivered in the first place I am not sure). For these reasons the statistical dimensionality reduction methods will probably remain relevant for some time.

There are dozens upon dozens of machine learning algorithms. There is the exotic sounding "support vector machine", a straight line drawer, and there is k-NN, which is a lasso type algorithm. Implementations of all of these algorithms are now easy to find for popular programming languages. One particular wavy line drawer is currently a particular favourite with AI researchers though and deserves a chapter of its own - the neural network.

Neural Networks

At the time of writing, neural networks (also known as ANNs or Artificial Neural Networks) are one of the most popular techniques for building a machine learning system and are often the default choice of algorithm in the most popular frameworks used by developers. Most of the leading edge impressive AI demonstrations, such as the latest generative AI, self-driving cars and chatbots are usually in some way now incorporating components built with neural networks. This is not to say that this is the final word in AI or that it is the most suitable method for any given application, it is just that the technique has seen a lot of success in sophisticated applications and is therefore a current focus of intense research.

Neural networks are a mathematical approximation of processes believed to go on in the human brain. The ideas are far from new, with the relevant mathematics being proposed in the early part of the 20th century. Work recognisable as current concepts started to come together in the 1960s and the prevailing modern method of training a neural network was first published in 1970 by Seppo Linnainmaa.[1]

Neural networks were always continuously researched but stayed somewhat under the radar until around the 2010s. The real development that made the technique favourable was the realisation that powerful and inexpensive commodity PC graphics cards intended for computer games (GPUs) could be co-opted to dramatically accelerate machine learning for this technique. It was just coincidental that there is a correspondence between the maths required for manipulation of 3D geometry and that needed for neural networks. This then inspired significant research progress in the field.

The basic unit of a neural network is the neuron which consists of a node with a number of input links and a single output link (see Figure 8). Each of the input links accepts a number (traditionally between -1 and +1). Each link has a "weight" attached to it, which is just another number. The input value to the link is multiplied by the weight and then passed to the node. The node totals all of the values emerging from the links after they have been multiplied by the weights on the links. Another optional value called a "bias" may be added to the total and then the result is sent along to the output link.

---

1   https://web.archive.org/web/20230405102651/https://people.idsia.ch/~juergen/linnainmaa1970thesis.pdf

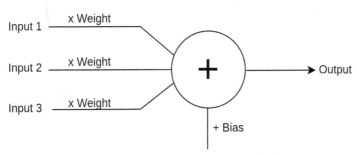

Figure 8 - A neuron showing three inputs, an output and a bias

After all of the multiplying and summing, the value on the output link may be outside the range of -1 to +1 and so a mathematical function is applied that re-scales the output number until it is within this range. This is known as the "activation function". There are several different possible choices for activation function and selecting the right one is somewhat part of the art of neural networks.

The output of the node may then be attached to the input of other nodes or might be the final output of the system. Commonly, the neurons are arranged in a grid structure (see Figure 9) however they do not have to be in this arrangement and some neural networks have other designs. The rows in the grid may have varying numbers of neurons and the number of links each neuron has can also vary. Quite often it is the case that every neuron is connected to every other on the preceding row but it is possible for the neurons to be connected in other ways.

The rows are known as "layers" and the neurons in the middle, that are neither inputs nor outputs, are known as "hidden layers". A system with only one layer is a valid neural network but suffers from certain problems such as difficulty learning nonlinear functions. It is rare to find a neural network in use that does not have at least two layers. Neural networks with many layers (at least three) are often described as "deep learning" systems.

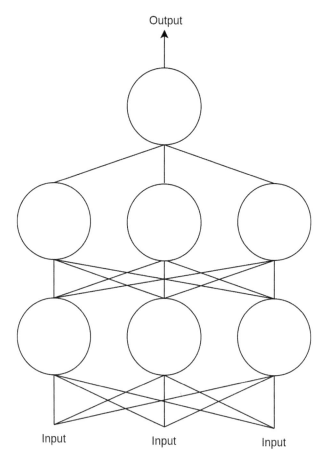

Figure 9 - A neural network consisting of three layers showing the neurons wired together

The structure of the network, the number of neurons in each layer and the number of layers is known as a "hyperparameter". This is a fancy way of saying something you just need to play around with to get it right. It's difficult to know up-front exactly how many layers will be needed or how many neurons, although an educated guess can be made through experience. Adding too few neurons may cause the system to fail to learn but surprisingly that is also the case with too many. A big brain doesn't always mean it will be smart. The more neurons are in a system, the longer it will take to train and the more expensive it is to run, so ideally the designer should prefer as few as is necessary to deliver good results.

The inputs are at the bottom of the grid and this is where the features arrive for the problem we are trying to solve. The input to the network might be the brightness of pixels in an image we are trying to recognise, the amplitude of samples in an audio signal or the temperatures recorded on several days that are being used to predict the weather.

In a common arrangement, each input is connected to each neuron on the first (bottom) layer but doesn't have to be. The input values are usually scaled such that they are in the range of -1 to +1. For example it is common in hardware for a camera pixel to be a brightness value represented by an integer between 0 and 255. This might be re-scaled such that 255 (maximum brightness) is represented by a 1 input to the neural network, 127 (half brightness) is represented by 0 and a minimum brightness value of 0 is represented by -1 in the network. It would be entirely possible to build a neural network that accepts other ranges, but -1 to +1 is commonly used.

Input data may also be pre-processed statistically to amplify the range of the data that contains the most useful information. For example in images it is common for the great majority of the pixel brightnesses to sit within a narrow band. The re-scaling of the inputs can take account of this and use more of the available -1 to +1 range of the neuron input to represent the range of brightnesses that are most frequent in the image. This exaggerates the differences between the pixel brightness levels that are most important to understanding the image and helps the machine learning system focus on this more important part of the range and learn more easily. For example if most pixel brightness values sit within a range of 100 - 150, but a few are outside this range, we might use most of the range of the neuron input e.g. -0.9 to 0.9 to represent the range between 100 - 150 and then everything outside of this range only receives a small amount of differentiation.

A form of pre-processing that has proven very helpful to image recognition happens in the "convolutional neural network". This arrangement passes a filter over an image prior to inputting it into the neural network, which often looks at a small 2D square of a few pixels (perhaps a 3x3 square totalling 9 pixels). The filter is mathematically exactly the same as those often found in image manipulation software (such as blur or sharpen) and works in exactly the same way.

The filter condenses the square of pixels down into a single pixel and this is what is fed into the neural network. The filter has the effect of generating a correspondence between adjacent pixels in 2D space. This is an improvement on just passing the pixels straight into the first layer of a neural network all in a long line. Deciding if a specific pixel is important to the subject of the photo depends on looking around at adjacent pixels in a two dimensional manner. The important correlated pixels are as likely to be above and below any specific pixel as they are to be to the left and right of it. The filter also operates in effect as a form of feature extraction, it might for example be performing some simple operation like edge detection. The filter is usually slid over the image in one pixel steps. The output of the filter may compress down colour information as well. So where the input image may have three separate dimensions for red, green and blue colour channels, the output may be a single continuous range (resulting in a value representing something like "chrominance").

The size of the first layer of the neural network that accepts the pixel inputs has a correspondence to the size of the input data. If the input is an image or audio, this can mean a large network. Even very cheap cameras can now have resolutions of 50 megapixels or more but this level of resolution is unnecessary to successfully recognise an image with high reliability. Reducing the size of the network will enable it to learn faster on cheaper hardware and the final version will also execute much faster. It is common for images to therefore be scaled down significantly before passing to a neural network. If the object to be recognised is relatively large in the frame, fairly small input images will often suffice, perhaps a size of only 256 pixels square will do the job. Similarly some applications can work perfectly well without colour and the image might be converted to grayscale which reduces the size of the network needed even further.

Audio can benefit from being pre-processed using a fourier transform which converts it into a list of constituent frequencies. From this, frequencies in the input that are not very significant may be removed which reduces the size of the input and helps remove noise that is not relevant to the task.

Decisions in a neural network are made by the weights on the links (with the bias). If a weight is large, then the relevant input has a large effect on the final output. If the weight is small, then the input being fed into the link has little impact on the output. In a system trying to predict the weather, it might learn that today's temperature has some impact on the temperature tomorrow, but the temperature recorded a week ago is of less relevance. So the input that receives today's temperature may end up with a larger weight which amplifies the effect of that specific input on the output. The temperature from a week ago may have a much smaller weight, it has some influence on the final network output but much less so.

The weights behave somewhat like taps controlling the flow of water, except in this case they are controlling the flow of information. When the network is trained, if a specific input seems to be useful for solving the problem, then the information flow from that input is turned up. If the input is less useful for solving the problem then the flow is turned down. So the training system attempts to adjust the weights in the appropriate direction to vary the relevance or impact that each input has on the output.

The optional bias can be helpful to give the neuron a tool to re-centre the output. Using only the weights a neuron might be stuck producing an output skewed towards one end of the range e.g. values of 0.8 - 1.0, but it would be more helpful to the next layer if it were moved into the middle of the range -0.1 to +0.1. The bias allows the neuron to add a constant value to shift the position of the output in the range of possible values. The bias is like an alignment adjustment setting as might be found on a projector to bring the image into the centre of the screen.

Of course, the big problem with neural networks is how do you know what to set the weights and biases to? Indeed, this was a conundrum for many years and wasn't immediately solved when the idea was originally conceived. Setting weights and biases is what "training" the neural network does. By far the most widely used (although not the only possible) training process is called "back-propagation". When the neural network first starts out, the weights and biases are often set entirely at random. The output of the network is therefore completely useless, or it would be an incredible coincidence if it wasn't. A training example is run through the network and it produces the output. The difference between what the network actually produced and what it should have output for the training example is calculated and is known as the "loss". There is some mathematical nuance to how loss is presented for best training effect but it is essentially the differential between the expected value and the value produced.

The training system then starts to methodically work backwards through the network (hence the name back-propagation), starting with the final network output and then the neurons at the layer before the output, then the neurons of the layer before that and so on until it reaches the input layer. For each neuron it calculates how much of a contribution that specific node made to the loss differential. If the neuron made a large contribution to a large loss then the weights of that neuron will get hammered right down as it's assumed that the neuron has no idea what it's talking about. Reducing the weights reduces the contribution that particular node can make to the output.

More training examples are then run through the network and the back-propagation learning technique tries to minimise the loss calculation to zero for all of the training data by gradually adjusting the weights relative to the contribution made to the loss. There is a parameter called "learning rate" that attempts to slow down the rate at which the weights are adjusted. This is to stop the network output from flailing around. For example it might wildly over-compensate in one direction, then wildly over-compensate in the other direction causing an oscillation in the output that never really settles down. The learning rate prevents the weight adjustment process from making rash assumptions based on a single training example and enforces that the training system will take a more considered and steady approach to learning.

After training, neural networks quite often end up self organising into a logical hierarchy. For example in a system intended to recognise faces, the first layer may be looking for edges (contrast changes), the next layer may combine those discovered edges into parts of faces: eyes and noses etc. Later layers may combine the parts of faces into the concept of a whole face. It's never quite that straightforward but generally finer grain components of the problem will be found on the lower layers nearer the inputs and more complete whole concepts are to be found encoded in the weights of the higher layers nearer the outputs.

Back-propagation isn't the only method of training a neural network. Another promising method that is worth a mention is "neuroevolution". This uses a technique called "genetic algorithms". This method works something like biological evolution. A population of many neural networks is initialised, largely at random. Each of the networks are tested for "fitness", that is test data is passed into the networks and the performance of the network against the test data is measured. By chance some networks will perform slightly better than others. The best performing networks are then "cross-bred" by taking some neuron weights from one high performing network and combining them with the neuron weights from another high performing network producing a new network. A new population of networks is produced in this way and retested. Then the best performers are cross-bred again and the cycle repeats. Gradually the network weights tend towards better performance.

Neuroevolution has the useful property that it can also be used to adjust the structure of the network as well as the weights. Currently network structure (such as the number of hidden layers) is largely hand crafted but it may be the case that in the future network structure is also machine learnt as well as the network weights and biases. So neuroevolution has the potential to get rid of hyperparameters or those unknowable numbers that you just have to play around with. A manually designed network structure and back-propagation is by far the current most popular method of constructing and training a neural network though.

Network structure is something that is not perfected and it is heavily researched. The exact organisation of neurons we have today for many problems may not be the optimal arrangement. In the future the organisation of neural networks might look quite different to how it does now.

AI Applications

Currently, there is no single generalised machine learning system that can be adapted to every task. Machine learning systems are split into a number of classes that have differing strengths. There is a great deal of overlap between the internal working of systems in the different groups and they are not completely dissimilar, but selecting the most appropriate style of algorithm for each job will lead to the best results. The following is a non-exhaustive list of some broad categories of machine learning systems and examples of tasks to which these systems may be applied.

Classifiers

Classifiers attempt to group data items by type and place them into buckets. A classifier might be used to decide if a photograph contains an image of a cat or a dog and sort the image files into appropriate folders. It can place all the cat photos into one folder and all the dogs into another. It might also be used to categorise pages of text by subject. All of the business stories in a newspaper may be placed into one category and all of the sports stories might end up in another category. More example uses for classifiers include:

- Spam detection and email categorisation: based on the words in a message is this email something the customer wants to read? Which department should this email be sent to?
- Authentication: deciding if a person is who they say they are based on their credentials and biometric data
- Customer segmentation: is this customer a high spender or a low spender? Should this customer receive a seat upgrade on a flight?
- Content moderation: deciding if user submitted content is within the policies of a web site
- Network traffic identification: what kind of information has a computer network just received from the internet? Where should the traffic be routed? Is the traffic normal or a threat?
- Natural disaster prediction: is a series of seismological readings an earthquake?
- Scientific data evaluation: astronomy can produce very large numbers of photographs with objects to be identified. Physics experiments can have large numbers of results that need to be inspected for anything novel.

- Crime prediction: predict which regions of a town might be subject to crime given a number of factors
- Music genre recognition: Is this music jazz, rock or classical?
- Satellite image analysis: millions of satellite photographs can be inspected to look for a missing aircraft, find a lost archaeological site or detect illegal logging.

Classifiers don't have to necessarily be particularly complicated pieces of software or in fact involve much in the way of machine learning. The following table is a perfectly valid classifier identifying coffee sizing, the rules for which are easily programmed. However, the classification problem is often more complex and machine learning software is needed.

Coffee Volume (fl. oz.)	Category
< 12	short
>= 12 < 16	tall
>= 16 < 20	grande
>= 20	venti

Most usually the classifier categories are pre-assigned. The developer of the machine learning system will manually label many hundreds of training images as pictures of cats or dogs. The system will be informed that there are two categories, called cat and dog, and then be shown all the examples.

It is also possible to persuade a system to decide the categories for itself, a technique often referred to as "clustering" which is a kind of "unsupervised learning". This might be useful with e.g. a batch of medical data. The developer can ask the system to group patients into categories based on blood pressure, weight and a variety of test results. The system is never explicitly told exactly how many categories of patients there are but decides itself how many logical groups make sense given the data. The system won't give the categories names, but can tell the developer ... ah yes, I can see three distinct groupings of patients in this sample. The developer can tune exactly how fuzzy the boundaries of the categories are which may cause the system to generate either more or fewer categories as appropriate.

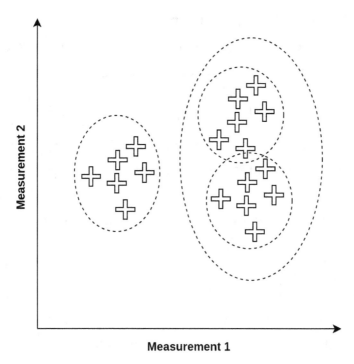

Figure 10 - Data points can be split into either two or three distinct groups based on how the parameters of the system are tuned

Classifiers can also generate probabilities as to how certain the system is that an image is one category or another. Instead of simply bucketing pictures into each category, it can say that it is 80% certain the image is a cat and 20% certain it is a dog. Probabilities might be used to trigger human review of the data. If the system is only 51% sure the image is a cat (and therefore 49% sure it is a dog), then the system has a significant degree of uncertainty. Without the probabilities being provided the classifier would put the image into the cat category, since it has the highest probability of being correct. The tiny difference between the probabilities in the two categories though means the system doesn't really know which category the image should go into, therefore the cat assessment could quite likely be wrong.

What the system is really measuring is the similarity of the test image presented to the training images. A very high probability in a single category with a low probability in all others means that the image is very similar to the training images. Where probability is more evenly distributed across the categories, then the image is likely more dissimilar to the set of training images and the system has a harder time telling them apart. The more training data the system has been given, the greater the distinction the system will be able to draw between the categories.

In many types of data, there exists the possibility that there may be more than one categorisation for the data item. For example, a photo may contain a picture of a cat and a dog, or perhaps it contains a picture of two cats. It is possible a news article might be about more than one topic. The first half of an article might be about the recent success on the field of a football club and then later in the article drifts into financial performance, viewing the club as a business. The article might therefore fit into the classes of both sport and business.

As well as assessing documents as a whole, a classifier can also automatically assess regions of a document. For example it can be tasked with pointing out where (if anywhere) in a photo a cat exists, then it may be asked to produce a probability that the area it is pointing at does in fact contain a cat.

Figure 11 - Bounding boxes highlighting multiple objects classified in the same image

Typically regions where the classifier has successfully found something are expressed as a rectangle (see Figure 11), as it is one of the computationally easiest shapes to deal with. When AI technology is shown in the media in relation to CCTV, a stereotypical depiction is a city street scene where boxes are drawn around the faces of pedestrians. This is a visualisation of the output of a classifier that has been tasked with locating human faces in the scene. The bounding boxes represent regions of the image that the classifier thinks might contain a face.

More complex shapes could be used and rectangles are not the only option. However for shapes that are not easily bounded in this way, a common technique is pixel level classification (or semantic segmentation). This produces a result like an image that has been painted over. A classifier is tasked with assessing which category each pixel in the image belongs to. A self-driving car might need to identify which regions of the image from a camera represent drivable roadways and which parts are pedestrian footpaths or cycle paths on which it should not drive. The area to be defined is often some amorphous region that would not be easily bounded by a rectangle, however the parts of the image need to be very precisely and sharply outlined as overlaps cannot be tolerated in this safety critical application. Pixel level classification is often used to paint the exact portions of the image that represent different classes of paving so it can identify where it may drive. The classifier is being asked for each pixel in the image, is this a road or a cycle path?

Classifiers can also be chained together. For example, one classifier might be good at identifying street signs. A bounding box identified might then be passed to another classifier that can identify exactly which street sign it is.

Regression

Regression is a cousin of classification with the difference that the system is usually attempting to predict the magnitude of a value instead of a class. For example a system may be tasked with estimating the price of a house from a variety of input variables (features). A real data set chose to use the following input factors as predictive of house prices:

- Number of rooms in the house compared with the average in the area
- Age of the property
- A measurement of pollutants in the local area
- The plot size the property was built on compared with the average in the area
- The distance to local centres of employment
- A value indicating the relative accessibility of major roads
- Local crime rate
- The student to teacher ratio in nearby schools

All of these factors represent an unproven hypothesis by the system developer as to features that may impact the value of a house. These factors all sound like reasonable things a prospective home buyer might consider, but some factors may be more important than others. The developer doesn't necessarily know in advance which features are the most important to buyers, however it would be useful information to a home builder to understand this information before committing to buying a plot of land.

Statistical correlation analysis can also be performed to discover which exact factors are most important. Do people mainly want good schools or is the home size most important? It's instructive to look at which way the correlation goes as it's not always obvious. For example with property age, are people interested in newly built properties or do older properties hold some charm? It's also possible to look at which factors are themselves related.

Regression systems are split into a number of categories, which include linear and non-linear regression, which relates to the nature of the relationship between the input variables and the output i.e. whether the system is a straight line drawer or a wavy line drawer. A non-linear regression system might have an easier time with variables that have a sweet spot. For example, do people prefer older homes, but they don't want them to be too old?

Regression can be converted into classification by placing the output values into buckets (like drawing a histogram). For example house prices might be classified as low, medium or high by setting prices to define the boundaries of each of those groups and then placing the regression outputs into the appropriate category.

Further uses for regression include:

- Risk assessment: given the size of a loan and the credit worthiness of a customer, predict the probability that a loan will be in default.
- Sales forecasting and inventory management: given the features of a product, the advertising expenditure and time of year predict how many units it might sell.
- Market analysis: given the age and income bracket of a customer, predict how likely they are to buy a product.
- Customer retention analysis: given the characteristics of a customer, what is the total expected profitability?
- Medical analytics: given the blood pressure and weight of a patient, predict the probability of some disease.
- Missing data completion: a table of information has some rows with missing values, use the completed rows to predict the values in the incomplete rows.
- Energy consumption: predict the energy consumption of a house based on time of day and the outside temperature.
- Transport planning: what is the rate of traffic flow depending on the number houses and offices built nearby?
- Insurance premium calculation: what premium should be charged based on the characteristics of the insured person?

- Agricultural yield estimation: given the soil type, expected weather and availability of water, predict the quantity of the crop that can be harvested.
- Quality control: given the hours of use of a machine tool and properties of the material it is working with, how many defects may be expected?

Sequence Predictors

Sequence prediction is a fundamental task in AI that involves predicting the next element or value in a sequence based on the patterns and relationships observed in the previously occurring historical elements of the sequence. For example, given a sequence of numbers, what is the next number in the list?

2 , 4, 6, 8, 10, 12 ...

A sequence predictor can work with considerably more complex and difficult to discern patterns. It can also predict several sequences at the same time. The system can work out what next value each of multiple sequences may have even where the sequences have complicated interdependencies.

The systems often work by trying to develop a mathematical function that describes the data in the sequence history. Once they have this function they can extend the sequence forever. For example, in the above sequence the system would be attempting to settle on a function of X + 2, where X is the previous number in the sequence. It can then continue to extend the sequence infinitely. A machine learning sequence predictor though can produce unfathomably complicated functions that would be exceptionally difficult for a person to discover by hand.

Sequence prediction is related to regression. It can be imagined a sequence predictor could be produced by making the inputs to a regression system the outputs it has just previously produced and asking it to predict one number at a time. Then you keep feeding the newly generated output value back into the input in a loop. This is a viable method but there are also specific sequence generating techniques that can have better results.

Sequence predictors have a lot of uses and regularly find applications in fields such as financial forecasting and medicine. Perhaps you would like to predict the future profitability of a company or perhaps you want to know the likely trend in blood pressure readings of a patient next week given the history of previous blood pressure readings? This is the kind of task that a sequence prediction system can help with.

As may be expected, the quality of the sequence prediction depends on if there is a pattern to be found in the data. It might fare better with medical data predictions than tomorrow's share prices. If the previous 10 years of share price history for Boring & Stable corporation is fed into a sequence predictor and the share price has been gently increasing in all that time, then that is what it will predict will happen forever. The sequence predictor doesn't know anything about the knowledge domain, it just sees the provided sequence and that is it. It doesn't know that successful companies tend to last a couple of dozen years and then decline because whatever market they serve changes. It doesn't know anything about "black swans" i.e. unforeseen financial events such as economic shocks. It doesn't expect a poor quality board of directors would ever be appointed or that the delivery of a substandard product would cause customers to depart. Neither the eventual explosion of the Earth's sun nor the end of the universe will stop the progress of Boring & Stable corporation's share price in the mind of the sequence predictor. It will increase forever.

The sequence predictor just predicts the sequence it has been shown. If the supplied historical data shows a gentle increase, then a gentle increase will be predicted and that is the mathematically correct outcome. The trick is to ensure the data it is shown is representative, accounts for all possible variables and that a prediction is reasonably possible.

One novel use for sequence predictors is content generation e.g. the production of music. A number can be assigned to each note in a scale e.g. C = 1, D = 2, E = 3 etc. Then music becomes a sequence of numbers that can be fed into a sequence predictor and the output is its guess at which note comes next. The sequence predictor can extend the music infinitely. The current "large language models" used in chatbots are also a form of sequence predictor, albeit a particularly sophisticated one with a quite different structure to a typical sequence predictor.

Recommendation Engines

Recommendation engines regularly appear in business contexts and can be a very valuable source of revenue. These are the kinds of systems that recommend products to customers based on past purchase history or perhaps recommend what you may like to watch next on a streaming video system. Recommendation systems are also used in advertising to attempt to assess which advert may be most of interest based on web pages viewed recently and customer demographics.

Supermarkets are often keen for you to have a store card so that they can record which products you buy against your email or postal address. They can then use a recommendation engine to try and discern which specific discount coupons to send you. The coupons are personalised to your shopping habits to try and entice you into the store.

There is a routinely told story in recommendation engine circles about a supermarket sending a woman a large batch of discount coupons for pregnancy and child products before she herself knew she was pregnant. The story sometimes comes embellished with an angry father confronting a beleaguered supermarket manager, who had nothing to do with the matter, about his daughter who had been sent all these vouchers. The story is probably apocryphal but supermarkets are genuinely very interested to know when someone is about to have a child as they usually spend a small fortune on baby products.

The video streaming service Netflix famously offered a million dollar prize to anyone who could beat its internal recommendations engine called "Cinematch". The system decides what customers may like to watch next based on what they have viewed previously. The company decided that this function was so valuable to them that they were prepared to offer a large prize for only a modest incremental improvement of about 10% in the performance of the system.

Massive successful businesses have been built on nothing but recommendation engines. The currently popular social media website TikTok is essentially little but a recommendation engine that helps users discover which videos to watch next and gradually learns the user's preferences and tastes. It then feeds them more of the videos it thinks they will enjoy and fewer of the videos they don't enjoy.

Anomaly Detection Systems

Anomaly detection systems are a kind of classifier that tries to decide if a particular action is something that happens normally or if it is something unusual. A popular application for this kind of system is in computer security, determining if an access to a system is by a trusted user or by some malicious third party. If you have ever received a CAPTCHA asking you to identify traffic lights or street signs whilst logging into a website, you have probably triggered an anomaly detection system. The anomaly detection system might be quite trivial, for example it may simply be detecting if you logged in from a different computer to the one you normally use. However it might also be a convoluted classifier system with very sophisticated behaviour looking at a wide range of signals.

Such systems are also used in financial fraud detection. Most credit card providers pass every single transaction through an anomaly detection system to see if each fits with the customer's usual pattern of spending. This is normally done very quickly in real time as the transaction is progressing. If the system is triggered you may receive a phone call in only a few minutes asking for verbal approval of a transaction or a notification in an app.

Generative AI

Generative AI is probably one of the most frequent types of AI that the general public directly encounters as it regularly hits the news headlines with impressive demonstrations from well funded companies with large marketing expenses.

Generative AI is that which produces creative content. For example it may generate a new unique image or video from only a description of what is required expressed in text form. Alternatively it may generate text to a user's specification based on an example prompt describing what is required. This form of AI product has come to particular prominence in recent years and it will be covered in more detail in subsequent chapters.

Optimisation Systems

Optimisation systems are presented with a black box. Some inputs go into the black box, perhaps there are some dials that can be adjusted, and a value comes out as a result of the settings on the dials. The optimiser is set the task of either maximising or minimising the output value and the system has to work out how to set the dials to produce the required output.

The goal might be to maximise the profit of a business for example and the dials might represent the price of products on the shelves. Set the price too low and profit goes down, set the price too high and customers become disgruntled and stop buying. There is an optimal pricing strategy somewhere in the middle.

Gaming and Autonomous Agent Systems

Computer games often need some form of antagonist character to challenge the player in order for the game to be fun. In older games the character behaviour was defined by simple programmed rules. If a player gets within a certain distance of the enemy then the character might be programmed to walk towards the player up to a preset distance and fire at them with a 20% chance of scoring a hit. Often these characters were not particularly intelligent, failing to notice the player if they were slightly beyond the programmed boundary, which acts like a tripwire. The enemy would just hang around somewhat uselessly and make little attempt to evade being hit whereas a real opposing player might dart back and forth, make attempts to hide behind cover and use some form of strategy.

Games have made various attempts to use AI driven characters to enable them to behave in more realistic ways as a real opponent player might. They can also gauge the skill level of the player in order to provide a challenging but not excessive opponent. Dynamically modifying the enemy to match the skill level of a player is often known metaphorically as "rubber banding", meaning that if a player becomes too far off target an invisible elastic band springs them back into the correct position. This is somewhat like the barriers in ten-pin bowling that assist unskilled players by bouncing the ball away from the gutter and back on target. The virtual bowling barriers in a game might have the effect of causing the enemy to be less accurate in its fire or fire less often than usual giving the player more time to react. Another technique is to provide the player with more useful bonus items if they are struggling and fewer if they are winning.

Game AIs can be trained through a technique known as "reinforcement learning", which is describing a goal to the AI and then providing it with feedback as to how far off target it was. A machine learning system works to try and minimise distance to the goal. With a singular main goal of "defeat the player", the system may not learn anything at all because the goal is too difficult to achieve for an unskilled bot and it rarely receives any positive feedback that it defeated the player. It only ever might win by pure accident. The bot needs regular incremental feedback that it is getting closer to the goal. To supply this it may be given a collection of subgoals that lead up to the main goal e.g. keep the player in its gun sights and minimise the number of times it is hit in a gaming session. It then scores points for how well it achieves those sub-goals. It has the ultimate aim of increasing the number of points it is earning.

Gaming AIs are more generally known as "autonomous agents" and the same kinds of techniques can be used to train robots operating in the real world as well. A robot can be trained to navigate around by using a goal and subgoals and providing feedback in the form of points as to how close the robot was able to get to achieving the tasks.

Audio Processing

Noise reduction is a common problem to which AI techniques are applied. A frequent application is to try and make speech more distinct. This has applications in video conferencing and computer games. A presenter may be in a noisy office with many background conversations going on and using a less than perfect microphone. The system attempts to cut out the distracting background voices and pick out only the voice of the main speaker, silencing all other sound giving the the impression they are speaking from a quiet room. This kind of technology would also be extremely useful if miniaturised in hearing aids, which tend to amplify all noise equally when the wearer wants to concentrate on the speech.

Beamforming is a technique related to noise reduction and aims to target sounds only from a specific 3D position. For example if there are several people talking simultaneously in a room, it aims only to concentrate on one speaker at a specific location. This is normally done using an array microphone, which is just a group of several microphones. It is possible to locate sounds by position from differences in the timing at which the same sound hits the different microphones. Beamforming is commonly used in AI voice assistants to improve the quality of speech of a speaker who may be far from the microphone prior to passing the audio to a speech recognition system.

Noise reduction can also be applied to other audio such as cleaning up old analogue music recordings and bringing the audio quality up to modern standards. A variation in music, which is a very similar problem to speech noise reduction, is audio segmentation. The main singer in an audio track can be extracted such that it can be placed over different music. It has been a common practice in music for decades to "sample" an artist, that is use a segment of one track within another. However, the point in the music where the original artist is singing may not have appropriate background audio. This can now be removed such that only the voice of the singer is present.

The inverse operation is also useful, where the singer can be removed leaving only the music. Karaoke systems have long attempted to do this with limited success, but the task can now be performed to a high standard using modern AI. It is also possible to target different parts of the music, for example extracting only a specific instrument. The bassline of a song can be extracted or only the drums. This can make remixes a lot simpler to produce or produce versions of music that a musician can play along with.

Echo suppression is a common problem in two-way audio communication, particularly where one of the participants in a conversation is using a speakerphone. The sound transmission is very slightly delayed and is picked up by the microphone and repeated back to the sender. It can often be very difficult to speak when there is an echo on the line. There are traditional methods for solving this problem but AI can do better.

Some kinds of sensors produce signals that are similar to audio and exactly the same processing techniques can be used. A vibration sensor produces a signal that is quite similar to a microphone. These sensors can be attached to monitor the safety of mechanical systems. We are all familiar with driving a car and hearing a sound that doesn't seem normal indicating there may be a problem. AI systems can listen out for unusual sounds in exactly the same way. Vibration sensors are commonly used in several places on aircraft. They are often used to warn that the rotation of a jet engine intake is starting to become eccentric and needs maintenance attention.

Noise reduction, echo suppression and beamforming are also useful in radio signal processing. All of these techniques are used in the transceiver in a mobile phone to improve signal quality.

Speech Recognition and Generation

Speech recognition systems transcribe spoken words into text. The technology has improved tremendously in the last few years, almost entirely due to neural network based learning techniques. High quality speech recognition is now available in all major languages and is now of a standard that is probably good enough for most applications.

Speech synthesis (converting text into speech) has been around for decades but up until recently the quality of the voice produced has been relatively poor. These systems used to rely on cutting together many voice samples, but there are too many possible ways in which one vocal utterance might transition into another with too many possible intonations to make this approach achieve high levels of realism. However, neural networks have again improved the technology and speech generation systems are radically improving. The technology is just on the edge of becoming indistinguishable from a recorded human voice. There are still issues with it but the current best generation systems are now quite good.

Once the generation of a high quality voice is a solved problem, there are still issues with automatically directing the voice output to be aesthetically appealing. Voice synthesisers tend to read speech in a monotonous, unemotional flat tone of voice, but this becomes tedious to listen to for any length of time and some variance in intonation is needed. To avoid sounding monotonous, the synthesiser needs to read the same words in a fractionally different manner each time.

For some applications, such as reading an audiobook, it is expected that the voice reads the text with a certain dramatic flair. This involves an understanding of the text being read. Should the text be read with energy and animation, with a bold voice, or perhaps whispered quietly? The system has to be able to understand the meaning and dramatic conventions for how text with a certain mood should be read.

There are also few character voices currently available. Most AI voices tend to be modelled after the style of a news reader. The voices are clear, pleasant and always in a sunny mood. However, works of fiction call for a wide range of characters. Different emotional states are needed for each voice, the voice might be happy, sad or angry. Some voices need to be younger and others older, some need to have foreign accents. Some require inflection in the voice, perhaps there is a need for a monster or a villain with a distinctive manner of speaking that sets them apart from other characters.

Machine Vision

Machine vision quite commonly refers to identifying objects in photos or video, which is a special case of classification. The input to the classifier is a set of pixels representing an image and the output is a label describing what is in the image such as "cat" or "dog". However, there are many other useful applications that are extensively studied within the field.

One problem is text recognition. Given a scan or photo of a printed or handwritten paper document, convert it into editable text for use in a word processor. The document may be printed in a variety of fonts and can have any conceivable structure. This process is often known as Optical Character Recognition (OCR) and is regularly used in business for storing customer correspondence in a searchable manner. It is also used for reading paper cheques in the finance industry or reading serial numbers on products on a production line.

Machine vision systems are used to understand data that has been specially constructed to aid a machine in reading it. The most commonly encountered examples are barcodes on products or QR codes. These data formats are specifically designed to reduce the complexity of the machine vision challenge and enable processing by relatively simplistic systems.

Determining the structure of objects in 3D space from a 2D camera or stereo pair of cameras is a useful task in computer graphics. For example, given a flat photo of an object it can be converted into a 3D model representation that can then be viewed from any angle. This process is known generally as "photogrammetry" and is already being regularly used to build 3D computer games. Systems that can achieve this have existed for some time based on mathematical techniques but more recently AI has been applied to the problem. The systems might often work from a collection of images taken from all around an object but equally it is technically possible to sometimes work from only a single image. Where a single image is used, this involves estimating what the reverse side of an object may look like. One advanced AI technique for achieving conversion of photos to 3D is called "NeRF" which stands for Neural Radiance Fields.

3D structure estimation is useful in the field of artificial reality, where a system attempts to merge computer generated objects with the real view through a camera and present the combined image to a user through a headset. Such systems might try to place computer generated images onto real physical surfaces. For example the user may place a computer generated character onto a physical coffee table that exists in the real world and the graphics react as if the character is actually present on the table. This relies on being able to understand where the surface exists in 3D space using only the view from a camera.

Another application from virtual reality is the opposite problem of positioning a headset or controllers in 3D space. There are many types of sensor that can perform this task, but one method is using AI driven machine vision. This is often known as "inside out" tracking. A camera is attached to a VR headset and the system uses the image to try to work out the distance the player is from walls in the room and the rotation of the camera across the three axes. This information is then used to work out where the user is in a 3D world and how to render the display.

Pose estimation attempts to calculate the position of a person's limbs using the view from a camera. Usually this results in a skeletal outline or stick figure of a person in 3D space. This process is useful for motion capture applications in the movie and games industries such that the pose can be transferred onto a computer generated character. Pose estimators can also be used as computer game controllers such that a person can wave their arms around in front of a camera to cause a computer game character to perform some action. Pose estimators can also be used as a form of remote control for a distant screen (such as a television) where the user cannot physically reach the monitor and so a touchscreen is of no use.

Image segmentation aims to find the boundaries of objects. For example, given a photo of a person, determine which pixels are the person and which pixels are the background. This is very useful in image manipulation software to be able to cut objects out of scenes and transpose them onto another background. The techniques are regularly applied in video conferencing software to blur, replace or otherwise obscure the background behind the speaker for privacy reasons.

Upscaling attempts to improve the resolution of video and is now a widely deployed application of AI, particularly in the field of computer games to produce better quality graphics with lower power hardware. Colourisation systems are also in use which attempt to bring old black and white video to life by estimating the correct colours.

Estimating the distance of pixels from a single or stereo pair of cameras is useful in the field of robotics to assist robots in navigating around environments in the way that humans do by judging how far away obstacles are. Calculating the orientation of objects from a camera image is very useful to industrial robots such that they can attempt to pick an item out of a basket by understanding the rotation (this is the "bin picking" problem).

Machine vision systems are used in industrial applications for inspection and quality control. For example a photo is taken of a circuit board as it passes along a conveyor belt and the system rapidly determines if all the required components are present on the board or if any have been missed.

Machine vision systems may use specialist cameras. Some of these cameras can see in wavelengths that humans cannot and are known as multi-spectral or hyper-spectral systems. Security cameras routinely use the infra-red band, which humans cannot perceive, to enable night vision outdoors without the need to shine a bright visible light that would disturb neighbours. Waste sorting machines often use these types of cameras to attempt to differentiate types of plastic which react differently to varying bands of the electromagnetic spectrum. The cameras are also used in food processing to identify foreign objects and improve product quality. Exactly the same image processing techniques may be applied to other bands, even if they are not visible to people.

Information Retrieval Systems

Information retrieval systems often aim to answer a question for a user. The most commonly used incarnation of this type of system is a web search engine. A user types in some keywords and the system aims to rank all of the web pages it has seen relative to how well they match the system's interpretation of those words. The system often doesn't precisely use the keywords entered but uses that as guidance to predict the underlying intent of the user.

Other types of information retrieval systems try to answer questions directly. The user enters a question as a full English sentence and the system attempts to find the answer e.g. when asked "What is the capital of Mongolia?" a traditional web search engine might answer with the Wikipedia page about the capital. A question answering system would attempt to go further. Some versions would try and highlight a paragraph that contained the answer. Other versions would attempt to respond with the precise response of "Ulaanbaatar".

Information retrieval systems can work with other modalities of information too though. A GIS (Geographic

Information System) might be interpreting a user's questions as a request to point out a specific location on a map. The system has to interpret the format of the address the user types and guess where it may be in the world, or else guess if it might be the name of a local business.

An image search system might interpret a photograph and try to explain what it can see. It might return either web pages that describe what it can see in the image or it might return other images that look like the photo taken. The user can then refer to the text on the pages where those images are found that presumably describes the photo. An image search system might work entirely the other way around and the system attempts to return an image that contains whatever the user typed in.

Graph based information search systems interpret information as a list of interconnected nodes and edges. These kinds of systems are often used on social media web sites to find friends. The system keeps a list of social relationships of the form Alice knows Bob and Bob knows Charlie. The system can then perform a search to suggest that Alice might know Charlie by linking through Bob. The system can use the graph to augment text searches. When Alice types in Charlie, the system knows she most likely means the Charlie associated with Bob and not some other person who is further away in the graph.

There are traditional methods for making these kinds of systems work, but AI techniques are increasingly being used to enhance the searches and deliver more nuance in the results.

Natural Language Processing

Natural language processing is computer processing of human written language. This is a tool that often acts as a component of other AI, such as information retrieval systems, by making human language easier for a machine to understand.

Tokenisation

Determining where an English word ends isn't quite as straightforward as it looks. It may be assumed that simply separating words out using any punctuation character would be sufficient and it is for quite a lot of sentences, but there are many exceptions. What about hyphenated words? What about contractions like don't where a single quote mark is part of a word, versus using single quotes to mark speech or quotations in text where the quote character marks the edge of a word? Sometimes people include several punctuation characters in a row like an ellipsis. English is actually one of the easier languages to tokenise into words, some languages do not even use spaces.

Similarly, finding the end of sentences is more difficult than it looks. It may be assumed a sentence ends with a full stop, but that is not always the case. What about initialisms such as I.B.M. or the decimal point in numbers? Lists often start with a number followed by a period.

Part of Speech Tagging

Part of speech tagging is the process of assigning a grammatical tag to each word in a sentence e.g. is it a noun, a verb or an adjective? The difficulty with this kind of tagging is that many words can serve in multiple grammatical roles depending on their context. For example, the word "run" can be a noun, as in "a morning run", or a verb as in "to run a race".

Homonyms are words that are spelt the same but have different meanings and often different parts of speech. For instance, "bank" can be a noun, a financial institution, or a verb meaning to tilt. Polysemous words have multiple related meanings and the part of speech can change based on the meaning in a given context. For example, "light" can be an adjective, meaning the opposite of heavy, or a noun as in illumination.

Language evolves over time, introducing new words and changing the roles of existing words. Part of speech taggers can struggle to recognise and correctly tag new terms or slang. Business language is particularly prone to nominalisation, that is turning verbs and adjectives into nouns (and also vice versa). There is also domain variability where the part of speech can change based on the intended audience of the text e.g., medical texts vs. news articles or the level of formality.

Stemmers and Lemmatisers

Stemming is the process of reducing words to their base or root form by removing prefixes, suffixes, and sometimes even parts of the word that indicate tense, plurality, or other grammatical variations. The resulting "stem" may not always be a valid word on its own, but it represents the core meaning of the original word. This helps a computer system look up a word by normalising it to the base meaning.

For example the word "running," "runs," and "ran" all have the same stem of "run." The aim of stemming is to group words that have similar meanings together, even if they have different suffixes.

Lemmatising is a more linguistically sophisticated process than stemming involving reducing words to their base dictionary form, known as the "lemma." For example "better" has "good" as its lemma.

Named Entity Extraction

A classic problem in text processing is "named entity extraction" where human written text (such as a news report) is read by a machine and it attempts to pull out a list of all the names of people it finds, the cities that are present or names of companies. It is possible to write a list of rules to do this job, for example, a word may be a name:

- If the word is preceded by a title or honorific from a list: Mr, Mrs, Miss, Ms, Dr
- If the name is capitalised in the middle of a sentence
- If the name exists on a list of known personal names

This approach can be reasonable and produce a moderately effective named entity extractor with only a few dozen rules. However, increasing the performance past a certain limit becomes difficult because of all the exceptions.

"Iris" is a female name, but also the name of a flower, a part of the human eye and the brand name of several commercial products which may be capitalised. It's difficult to know which is meant without a proper understanding of the language. There is no comprehensive list of all world names. Foreign names may not exist on a list compiled for a specific language. The start of a sentence is always capitalised but a name to be extracted may appear at the beginning of a sentence. Some text may contain typos and a name that should be capitalised may not be capitalised. A human reader is usually able to handle these errors and a machine should be able to do this too.

Machine Translation

Machine translation is the translation of one human language into another through software. This is a technology that has been improved dramatically in recent years using the latest neural network techniques.

Older versions of machine translation often worked with large phrase lookup lists (like dictionaries), replacing recognised phrases with those from the other language. More recent systems use a matched pair of machine learning converters. One knows how to translate the source language into an intermediate form that encodes the raw meaning of the text. The other machine learning system knows how to convert the meaning of the intermediate language into the target language. It's somewhat like the idea of pivoting through a special constructed common language such as Esperanto.

Summarisation

Summarisation systems attempt to reduce the size of a piece of text whilst maintaining as much of the meaning as possible and still ensuring that the text makes grammatical sense. A target word count may be the set that the summariser aims to work within.

Sentiment Analysis

Sentiment analysis determines the general emotional mood of a piece of text. Is the text expressing a positive or negative sentiment for example? This kind of analysis has a number of applications in business, for example customer emails can be redirected appropriately depending on if the text seems to be a complaint.

Social media feeds for large companies often contain exceptionally large numbers of responses that would be difficult to sort through by hand. Sentiment analysis can be used to determine if the general mood of the responses is positive or negative and chart how customer perception of the company is drifting over time. This can form part of a brand reputation monitoring system.

Conversational Systems

Conversational systems attempt to be able to converse with a user interactively in natural language as opposed to a machine or special language. These are systems such as chatbots. The systems are currently mainly based around generative AI and will be covered in the large language models chapter.

Data Compression

The field of data compression has a great deal of crossover with machine learning. Data compression is widely used in computer science to reduce the size of files. The most commonly encountered consumer facing examples are the "zip" format frequently used on personal computers but more regularly video, audio and image compression. There is practically no media sent over the internet or any wireless transmission that is not compressed in some way to reduce the transmission cost. The venerable MPEG layer 3 format (more commonly known as mp3) enabled the transmission of music over the low bandwidth home connections of the 1990s which was previously impractical. The format was originally designed with the intent of delivering reasonable audio quality over an ISDN phone line.

Data compression works by either trying to find common elements in data files and removing the redundancy or else trying to remove information that the user will not miss. The latter approach is known as "lossy" data compression as the reconstructed result is not absolutely identical to the original but near enough. Most media is compressed using lossy techniques. Experts and audio aficionados may disagree, but the general public cannot usually tell the difference between an original signal and a lossy compressed version and this is why the technique is so popular. It is sometimes known as "perceptual" compression as-in the average human does not perceive a difference even though there is technically a difference.

The construction of an AI model often naturally results in a form of lossy data compression as the model contains the "essence" of the original data in some form. As generative AI shows, something like the original form can be reconstructed from the model. There are various attempts and experiments to use AI techniques to try and produce better compression methods than the current algorithmic compression techniques such that smaller files can be produced with less human perceivable loss.

Routing Systems

There are many problems that involve trying to find the best route from one location to another. This is quite a challenging problem to solve using traditional computation because of the number of permutations in the route that are possible and the constraints.

The most obvious example is a satnav system that attempts to find the optimum route to drive from one place to another. The shortest route may not be the best route as some roads have higher speed limits than others. The level of traffic on each road also affects the best route and the traffic may be different at different times of day. In some applications the route may need to pass through a set of waypoints, such as in package delivery.

Robotics has many similar routing problems where a robot must work out how to travel from one location in a space to another whilst avoiding obstacles. It must decide if it can successfully fit through a gap and how it must orient itself to do so. It may also need to work with moving objects, such as people, vehicles or other robots, estimating the trajectory of the moving object and where it may soon be to avoid bumping into it.

Electronic circuit design is replete with routing problems with competing constraints. Software has to work out how to wire up components on a 2D plane and get the connections past each other without overlapping. Some components benefit from being close together to minimise transmission delays. Some components might need to be far apart to avoid electrical noise. Some components might need to be at the edge of a board and only located on a particular side such that a connector can be installed through a plastic case. Some components might have a specific orientation, such as a display. The smaller the board that can be used, the cheaper the product is to produce and the more portable the product can be.

Training Data

Acquiring high quality training data is one of the most important aspects of machine learning, and also one of the most difficult parts of the process. The technology behind a machine learning system may be sophisticated, but without a large quantity of good quality training data it becomes completely useless. The training data is the teacher. If the teacher isn't any good, then it doesn't matter how intelligent the student is.

There are continuously improving techniques for reducing the amount of training data that is required for any given application but currently the rule of thumb is the more training data that is available, the more effectively the system will be able to learn and the higher the quality of the resulting model. There will be a point of diminishing returns, but generally more is better.

Understanding exactly how much data will be needed to produce a model that is good enough for the intended application is not yet a refined science, it is somewhat of an art. Determining the right amount of data is a case of trial and error and seeing how well the model performs. If the results are insufficient then additional data may be needed. A classification system using current technology is likely to need many thousands of examples to operate effectively under all conditions.

Acquisition of training data can be very time consuming and expensive. An organisation may need to licence a large amount of data and possibly also (but not necessarily) employ rooms full of people to label data with the relevant categories for the system to learn. If the field is specialist, such as medicine, the relevant expertise to produce the training data set may be in short supply and also expensive.

Avoiding Overfitting

A machine learning system might learn the training data almost perfectly, however the developer may find the learning is not sufficiently generalised. The system may have picked up on some feature peculiar to the training data, but the thing it has noticed is irrelevant to the concept it is trying to learn. Alternatively it may have just learned all the examples in the training data but doesn't actually understand the abstract concepts it is supposed to be comprehending. These kinds of problems are known as "overfitting".

This is somewhat like a student memorising facts by rote but never actually learning the concepts around the information. When the student is presented with examination questions, they cannot answer them because the questions are not absolutely identical to the material they learnt from. The student is unable to generalise from the training material and apply the learning to a different situation.

One way to help avoid this problem is splitting the training data into two parts. One part of the data is used for training the machine learning model and the other part is unseen by the machine learning system and acts as an exam that it must pass. This is often known as the validation or test set. The unseen part of the data is then used to regularly test the model to ensure it is in fact learning the abstract concepts and not just memorising the information or employing some other method of cheating and avoiding learning the actual concepts.

If the system seems to be failing its exam there are a number of things that may help. Introducing more training data can work. This method can disrupt whatever cheating technique the model has latched onto. Attempting to eliminate features in the data that are not likely to be relevant to the learning process can sometimes help. That is, demonstrating to the student what it is you want it to focus on. This is known as feature selection. There is also a related method called regularisation that attempts to reduce the amount of noise in the training data set which clarifies the important aspects.

Augmenting Training Data

Training data for machine learning systems is often hard to acquire and there is not enough to be found. There may be plenty of photos of cats available on the web but not many photos of an obscure electronic component that you want an industrial robot to classify. Some subject matter can be surprisingly sparse on the open web with only a few good quality images to be found. There are also problems with the copyright of training data acquired from public sources, which haven't been fully resolved.

One method of solving this is to take whatever training is available and then attempting to modify it to manufacture additional derivative training data. For example there are many image transformations that can be applied to a photo to produce a new photo (see Figure 12). An image can be rotated through several steps. Most photos are usually originally taken the right way up, but it may be helpful for the recognition system to be able to identify the object upside down. The image can be mirrored, if it still makes sense for the system to learn it backwards. It can also be scaled or expanded. The image contrast can be adjusted and so can the colour levels to simulate varying lighting conditions. Image kernel transformations can be applied (blur filters or sharpen filters) to simulate variations in the quality of the camera the image was taken with. These are all transformations that are very simple to apply with easily available software and can significantly bulk out training data to help make the system more robust.

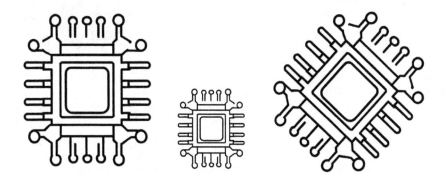

Figure 12 - Training images scaled and rotated

Another technique is to deliberately degrade image quality, which can improve the model stability and is also another technique for reducing overfitting. Easily available image filters can add noise to the image and regions of the image can also be deleted at random (replaced with a black rectangle or other shape). A human can usually recognise an object even if it is partially obscured, and hence obscuring the image can help improve the machine learning model (see Figure 13).

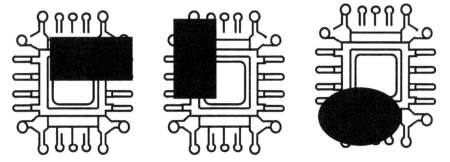

Figure 13 - Sections of image removed at random

For text based data it can be possible to cut the same text together in various different orders. For example if the problem is to recognise the subject of news articles, the articles can be split into paragraphs and rearranged into different combinations or paragraphs from one article mixed with another.

It can also be possible to use templates and write a simple program to fill out the templates with a list of alternative words. For example, if the articles contain names of cities and that is not relevant to the machine learning problem, the cities may be swapped out from a gazetteer with other place names which will help prevent the AI from latching onto that particular feature in its learning. A thesaurus can be used to automatically replace words with synonyms.

As with images, text quality can also be degraded. This can be achieved with a simple program that occasionally inserts random words into training data or deliberately replaces words with spelling mistakes. Alternatively, words can be deleted at random from the training data to vary the data quality and improve the robustness of the machine learning system to error.

Audio training data can be augmented by changing the speed, pitch and amplitude of the samples, which is fairly easy to do en masse with easily available audio software. The bandwidth of samples can also be easily reduced to produce the effect of the sample sounding like it is played through a telephone. Audio noise (like tape hiss or mains hum) can also be added to degrade samples. Background sounds from pre-existing audio effects libraries can be mixed into otherwise clean audio. The sound of commonplace daily activities such as a car horn or background chatter can be mixed into speech recognition training samples to persuade the system to ignore this kind of noise and concentrate on the speech.

Some popular machine learning frameworks employed by AI developers now include data augmentation systems as standard and can automatically bulk out the training data using the above set of techniques.

Adversarial Training Data Augmentation

A machine learning system can be used to generate augmented training data with the deliberate intent of attempting to make a classifier produce the wrong result. A high quality test example is passed to a classification system e.g. a cat detector is passed a good image of a cat that it reliably identifies as a cat with high probability. Another machine learning system then attempts to just slightly modify the image until the classifier fails to detect the image as a cat. This may be done by adding small amounts of noise to the image.

The classifier is re-trained until it correctly identifies the modified image as a cat again. The malicious machine learning system is then put to work again to find a different very slight modification to the cat image that again causes the cat detector to fail and the classifier is re-trained until it works again. This process is repeated in a loop until the malicious machine learning system cannot find any more minor modifications to the image that cause the classifier to fail.

Simulated and Synthetic Training Data

For some problems it may be possible to bulk out training data by use of a simulator. This technique has been widely applied to self-driving car data sets. A simulation of a real world environment, similar to a computer game, is built and the system is trained on video data derived from the simulation. Simulations that are possible these days can be exceptionally high quality and almost indistinguishable from real images. However it is often not necessary to produce an image of such fidelity. Something quite modest can produce useful training results.

The learning that the system can perform via the simulation is transferable to the context of a view of the real world through a video camera. Training on real world images is still required, but much less real photographic image training is subsequently needed after first using the simulation.

People can sometimes learn in exactly the same way. Commercial airline pilots are often trained on simulators because it is so expensive to fly the actual aircraft. The learning from the simulator is transferable to the real aircraft even though the experience is not precisely the same. The pilot most definitely needs practice in the real aircraft, but much less practice is required after using the simulator.

Sometimes a complete and accurate mathematical model of the boundaries of the task can be feasibly constructed in a simulator but learning how to perform the task is difficult. For example, teaching a robot how to walk is a very difficult task. However a simulator can be constructed that contains all the relevant laws of physics. The robot then learns from the rules in the simulator how to perform the task. This approach is used in reinforcement learning. A simulated robot is awarded points depending on how well it performed at the required task. For example it might be rated against how far it travelled balanced against how little energy it used and a competing aim of how quickly it performed the task. A machine learning system would be tasked with maximising the points by trying out different methods of walking. The training data is effectively encoded in the rules programmed into the simulator as opposed to providing the robot with specific labelled examples of how to walk.

Often the simulator needs to be iteratively refined as the machine learning system learns to exploit bugs in the simulator and game the system. The robot might end up flying instead of walking because the rules about gravity have not been correctly codified. The reinforcement system seeks to maximise points by any means it can, which is not necessarily as the programmer intended. The machine learning system can in effect help to debug the simulator.

Another interesting avenue that has appeared is the use of generative AI techniques to enhance training data volumes by producing synthetic data. Generative AI is the kind of now widespread products that can create images, text or video from supplied text prompts. Usually these systems can produce an unlimited number of examples on request. There are however limits to the creativity of the systems and the training data produced is going to be reflective of the training data that the generative AI has itself seen. The outputs are also not free of errors, which will then introduce those same errors into the model that is trying to learn from it. Generative AI can be a shortcut to producing a large amount of training data by gaining a boost from the, often considerable expense, that has gone into training the generative AI system. Real training data will still however be needed to avoid the biases inherent in the synthetic data.

New AI techniques are also available that can transform images, these can be used like filters to produce new variations of images in different styles to augment the training data set. For example a photograph can be converted to the style of an oil painting through "style transfer". This can be used to bulk out training data sets with lots of different variations of the same photo.

Unsupervised Training Sets

Sometimes obtaining training data in bulk is not the problem but labelling it all is an issue. Millions of items of data might be scraped from the web using a simple robot in a few hours at near zero cost, but employing a room full of people to categorise the data would cost a fortune and take weeks. Some forms of machine learning problems are suited to unsupervised techniques. This is where no labelling of data is needed but just a lot of training data is required.

Clustering is a form of unsupervised learning. This is where a system is just given some data and asked to segment it in some way. For example a system might be given a batch of customer sales data and can split it into logical groups, each representing a particular type of customer or market segment. The system is never told explicitly how many types of customer exist.

A question answering system can be constructed by downloading lots of web pages that might contain useful facts (for example Wikipedia is a source of web pages rich in facts) and then asking the machine learning system to play a game of completing the missing word. The text is split into paragraphs and parts of the text are redacted at random. The machine learning system is then asked to guess the text that has been blanked out. For example, the machine learning system might be asked to guess the missing word in these randomly redacted versions of the same sentence:

The ****** of France is Paris.
The capital of ****** is Paris.
The capital of France ****** Paris.
The capital of France is ******.
****** capital of France is Paris.

Most instances where a word is blanked out are irrelevant and contain no useful answers, but by a scattergun approach, many of the instances will also be the answers to questions and the system will be learning to provide those answers. It will also learn to get good at providing irrelevant information, but that behaviour can be screened out by controlling how the system is used through software.

Harnessing Wasted Human Effort

A clever technique for generating labelled training data is to make use of human effort that would otherwise go to waste. CAPTCHAs are, often irritating, boxes that appear on the web when performing some action. The boxes might ask you to locate the position of a traffic light in a photo or determine what a house number says. CAPTCHA stands for Completely Automated Public Turing test to tell Computers and Humans Apart. The purpose of these boxes is to prevent a robot from accessing some resource. For example it may be used to try and prevent a robot from creating an email account, where the company providing the service only wants it to be available to humans.

Initially CAPTCHAs would display some form of distorted text that was difficult for a robot to read but (somewhat) easier for a human to read. The human effort involved in the task was largely wasted and the task did nothing other than keep the robots out. However it was subsequently realised that CAPTCHAs could be used to provide training data for machine learning.

CAPTCHAs started to be used to digitise historical newspaper archives from paper such that they could be made searchable on the web. A high quality OCR (machine reading) system was passed over a scan of a newspaper page. The OCR system would report which words it was unable to read. The unknown words were then passed to users as CAPTCHA tasks challenging them to prove they were not a robot by typing in what the word says. By definition, the scanned words delivered to users are data items that the best robot in the business could not decipher, therefore someone who can complete the task must be a human. To verify that the human did in fact complete the task and didn't just type in nonsense, the CAPTCHA user is typically presented with two words. One word the system already knows the answer to and the second word is unknown. The system doesn't tell the user which one is which, forcing the user to type both words to pass. If the user fails on the known word then they are a robot or a malicious user that is not completing the challenge correctly. The same scan is also typically passed to more than one user to confirm they give the same answer to the challenge.

The newspaper archive now has the missing words filled in, which is one useful task, but also the scans are passed back to retrain the robot with the correct answers now fully labelled up. The robot can then get better at scanning the newspapers. Eventually the scanning problem is solved and the OCR system doesn't need humans anymore. At which point we move onto a different type of CAPTCHA challenge and improve some other aspect of AI.

CAPTCHA services are offered for free as there is a mutual business benefit proposition. A website owner who wants to keep robots out of their service receives the benefit of the free software development that went into the CAPTCHA and also free use of the servers on which it runs. The CAPTCHA developer gets the resulting data which can be sold to an AI company to pay for the service.

Another novel approach that has been successfully used is the gamification of AI training data labelling. People often like to play games, but the actual effort going into the game is usually wasted potential. What if playing the game could be used to train an AI that has commercial applications?

One example was a popular game intended to label images with descriptions of what the image contained. Two randomly chosen players were both presented with the same image and asked to type words describing the image content. When the players both typed the same word, they scored points. Two randomly chosen, independent users with no ability to collude who enter the same word means there is a good chance that it is a valid description of the image. Once the system had collected enough verifications of a particular image description, it would present the image but with a list of "banned" words that the game player was not allowed to type. This would be a list of descriptions of the image that the system was already highly confident were correct, to try and persuade the players to come up with additional varied descriptions of the images.

The gamification approach has a number of limitations. People need to find the game fun and many AI data labelling tasks may not be easily convertible into fun. Also the game needs advertising and people have to be encouraged to play it. Creating a hit game is not an easy proposition and it is more luck than judgement as to whether a game becomes successful. The popularity of games also waxes and wanes and people get bored and look for a new distraction. Gamification is not really a reliable or widely applicable approach, but is another tool that is available for generating data.

The CAPTCHA approach benefits from essentially a captive audience in that people cannot avoid completing the task if they want the service it is gatekeeping. However, the gamified approach is more hit and miss as to whether people can be persuaded to play it. Gamification might be useful in a corporate environment where people are paid to label data. This can be a mind-numbingly boring task with high staff turnover where even the payment isn't enough incentive to do the task for long. Gamification might help keep paid employees engaged.

Recycling an Existing Model

Sometimes an existing model can be found that is somewhat like the task you want to do but is not exactly right. If such a model can be found, this can dramatically reduce the amount of training data that is needed. For example if you were looking to build a tiger detector and were unable to find one, a good starting point may be a pre-existing house cat detector.

You are much more likely to be able to find a model of a house cat detector just because it's a popular photographic subject. Everybody and their dog has a house cat - well maybe dogs are less enthusiastic - but lots of people have cats. This means there are many millions of photos of the humble moggy on the internet which means a vast array of training data is to be found. The tiger though is an endangered species and owners of tigers would be similarly endangered. Tiger photographers will sometimes have gone to some expense and difficulty to obtain their photos but cat photographers will have been caused considerably less trouble. Consequently there are fewer tiger photos which means less training data. Looking on a popular image search engine, there are currently about 80 easily available high quality photos of tigers but the list of house cats goes on forever. A set of 80 tiger photos might not be enough to get a good result out of a classifier.

An existing model for a similar task will likely have already become good at detecting the kinds of features you are looking for. It will already know about ears and tails and whiskers, what it may be missing is the concept of orange stripes. However, by starting with an existing model in the same domain, far fewer training examples will likely be needed before it will also get good at detecting tigers. This is somewhat like the idea of emergent complexity delivering n-shot learning (except you may need more than a couple of examples). This idea is covered in more detail below.

n-Shot Learning

The terms zero-shot, one-shot and few-shot learning (collectively n-shot) refer to the concept of a system being able to learn with little or no training data at all. When a toddler learns, it doesn't usually take a lot of examples before it manages to pick up a concept. A mini-person that has never seen a cow before may only need to see a picture once or twice before they understand the concept and can successfully recognise a cow for ever more.

Zero-shot learning means the system just knows the concept anyway even though a training example may not have been particularly highlighted to it. One-shot learning means a single example will do and few-shot refers to the capability to learn from considerably less training data than has been traditionally needed, perhaps just half a dozen examples or less.

There has been a lot of research as to how to get n-shot learning to work, but it seems like it may be an emergent property of complexity. When a machine learning system reaches a particular size and has seen a certain number of examples, it just starts to get good at n-shot learning entirely naturally. The system starts to need fewer and fewer examples to understand a new concept. So n-shot learning might just be something that arrives for free as a result of the depth and complexity of machine learning systems improving and no real special coding is needed. N-Shot learning is really a similar concept to recycling an existing model. The models seem to provide progressively more benefits the larger and more complex they are.

Large language models are proving particularly good at few-shot learning. The larger the model, the better it is. The models have not been specifically informed how to do few-shot learning, the capability has just appeared.

Some systems have been explicitly set-up to do few-shot learning. There are now speech synthesis systems that can mimic a specific voice using only a few seconds of audio rather than needing hours and hours of input. The way these are working is more the case that the systems have heard a considerable number of distinct voices and are performing a search to find the relevant parameters in their database that are similar to the target voice. The system may be presented with a voice, it determines that it is Scottish, male, 60-years old and some other parameters that are harder to describe. It has heard examples of a Scottish accent before, a 60-year old voice and a male voice, but perhaps not all at the same time in the same training example. The system is however able to draw these elements together and synthesise a new voice that sounds somewhat similar to the input example. The system did not learn to mimic the original voice as such, but just had so many example voices on tap that it could perform a search to find all of the elements it needed and then seamlessly weave the component parts together to get close to the required voice.

The very largest of models that are now appearing can act as a form of baseline where a wide variety of other tasks can be added on top with only a small sprinkling of training data needed. These large models are now sometimes known by the term "foundational models" due to this capability of behaving as a platform on which additional training can be built.

Feature Selection

One large and well capitalised company in the property listings business had the idea that they would buy undervalued houses, renovate them and resell them for a higher price. Renovating and reselling houses is of course not a novel business idea, there are armies of competitors already involved in the space and the practice even has a name - "flipping". However, the company thought they would be able to add a new twist to the business model and do a better job. They would use AI techniques to discover the most undervalued properties that would yield the greatest profit margins and also be able to accurately predict the price in several months after the house was renovated. They would often not even send anyone to look at the property in person and make an offer to the buyer over the web. As we saw in the AI applications chapter, a regression model could be suitable for this problem.

Unfortunately, it did not work out, the company went on to lose hundreds of millions of dollars in only a few months.

In some areas they were listing almost all purchased homes at a lower price than they originally paid.

There could be a general problem with the business model. AI could be perfectly good at estimating house prices but people are pretty good at it as well and the AI perhaps cannot provide a sufficient market advantage to make the transaction as a whole more profitable compared with all of the other competition and doesn't add any extra value. The actual task of estimating the value of a house isn't a large part of the cost of flipping a house and doesn't necessarily benefit from automation. Getting the correct valuation, by whatever means, is most important.

Many small-scale house flippers are using their own personal labour to renovate the houses, whereas the corporate version has to pay for various tradespeople to do the work in addition to someone to manage the whole job and designers to decide how the house will be renovated. The former may accept less money for their efforts versus the combination of property professionals and hence be able to offer a more competitive deal on the house overall which drives out the profits from the large-scale version of the business.

Some attributed the failure to "black swan" events, these are significant market occurrences that are difficult for any model to forecast. If you are buying houses with borrowed money, a sudden swing in interest rates is a black swan event that can make your venture immediately unprofitable.

Interest rate changes are notoriously difficult to precisely forecast despite a lot of people working on the problem.

Others though, including somewhat tacitly the company themselves, attributed the issue to the machine learning failing to correctly forecast the house price. The company described this issue as "market volatility" which is another way of saying they failed to accurately predict future prices, which was exactly what the model was intended to do. This was compounded by a desire for rapid expansion leading to the company making higher than necessary offers. Using the AI models they were so sure that the property was a steal, they would offer a little extra to the vendor to get the deal done quickly and expand market share. However, the value in the property turned out to be not as great as the model suggested.

Subsequent companies have been able to make a success of machine learning house buying, which suggests perhaps there is something in the idea and it does work to some extent. It may be the case that other companies just have better models. The difference is unlikely to be in the actual machine learning technology as such, the difference is likely in the original hypothesis on which the model was based. The cheap houses were cheap for a reason and the company didn't have the relevant features in their model to understand exactly why they were cheap. The local estate agents [realtors] intuitively knew about the factors that were most important in influencing the price, hence the original pricing was actually accurate and the selected homes were not undervalued at all.

I recall seeing a nice looking house advertised for sale at a low price but with an unusually closely cropped photo - always suspicious. On taking a look at the house in person, the problem was immediately evident. High voltage power lines went straight over the top, just feet above the roof. Would the designers of an automated house pricing AI model have had the foresight to include a map of power line locations in the original set of features that they believed influence the price of a house? If not then they may have perceived this house as being a great value buy, when it was actually more fairly valued and less profitable. The correspondence between power lines and house prices is more complex than distance from the house. If there is a hill or other obstruction in the way of the lines and the house then there may be no issue at all, it's the line of sight to the power lines that is important and so topographical information may be as relevant as the distance to the lines.

To build a good machine learning model it is essential to start with a good hypothesis underpinning the important features pertaining to the problem. In the above case, an understanding of what factors affect the price of a house. If the hypothesis is wrong or incomplete, the machine learning model will be useless. This is a matter for domain experts as much as it is for computer scientists. Input from property experts might be needed to determine what factors they consider relevant when making decisions.

Factors that are thought to be important but later turn out to be of no use can often be weeded out statistically and don't typically do any damage to the quality of the model as the systems are usually smart enough to detect useless features. So you may as well try and test a lot of theories. There are some caveats around that assertion though. One problem is spurious correlations that can turn up. The machine learning systems will find correlations between system inputs and outputs but some human judgement is required as to whether the correlations make any logical sense. The more features that are included in the input to a model, the higher the risk of a spurious correlation occurring.

There are internet forums dedicated to finding spurious correlations between variables for comedic value. These correlations include such gems as goals scored by a particular football player influence the rate of inflation or that sales of a specific fruit predict global monetary exchange rates. Each of these correlations comes with a highly convincing chart showing a flawless correlation between the variables. Of course, applying some common sense, it makes no sense for such a correlation to exist.

Politics is a domain in which the spurious correlation is converted into journalistic currency: no electoral candidate younger than the age of 50 has ever won in this area. The spurious correlation is just a way of obtaining some form of prediction of the future to fill air time during the vote counting. The outcome is unknowable and won't emerge for several hours but the rolling news needs something to fill the void. Talking heads can be drafted in to make guesses as to why it may be that this area doesn't like younger candidates and come up with a perfectly reasonable sounding hypothesis. When a 49 year-old wins, the narrative for the next election moves on to some other spurious correlation and the original assertion is forgotten.

The reason these correlations occur is if you take a large number of sequences of arbitrary metrics, there are a large number of possible combinations of those sequences and there is a high chance two of them will happen to flawlessly align by random chance. If you wait a while longer, the statistics will eventually diverge and the correlation will prove to be false over the long term. Within the time frame of the machine learning training data though, a correlation may exist and the system will dutifully find it even if it makes no logical sense.

Another such spurious correlation is ice cream sales are related to the frequency of shark attacks. In this case the correlation sounds nonsensical but it is actually a true correlation that stands the test of time. However, it's a case of the right idea but with the wrong reasoning - there is a 3rd factor at play. Hot weather brings more people to the beach, increasing the risk of someone being bitten by a shark and hot weather also causes an increase in the sales of ice cream. The relevant aphorism is "correlation is not causation". The caution that needs to be exercised is to analyse the model and find out which factors it is mostly relying upon and then think through if a connection between the input and the output makes logical sense. There is a correlation, but banning ice cream won't do much to ward off sharks.

Adding more features also increases the risk of "noise", that is features that contain errors. Not all data arises from flawlessly reliable sources and adding features with noise might introduce correlations with the mistakes. Most data contains some errors which a machine learning system can usually successfully ignore as long as there is enough good data, but large numbers of errors and particularly systematic errors could be problematic. For example if one data source for housing has consistently mislabeled the floor area column as metres squared instead of feet squared and every input in the data is wrong, that would produce an inaccurate model. Such an error might be easily found, but other data errors might be a lot more subtle.

Bias is another problem in feature selection. People might (and probably do) have preconceived ideas about which input factors are correlated with an output. It may be the case that the wrong features have been chosen and no correlation emerges. Someone may discount a feature due to their own view but with a different perspective added into the mix, it may be that the true correlation is to be found against a different set of features. It's therefore important to obtain a diversity of ideas, especially where there are divergent expert opinions in a field.

Sometimes it is not always easy to get all of the required information. A home vendor probably knows something that they don't want to reveal, but there may be factors that leak information about the hidden knowledge that they have. This might be important to include in the model. In the previous example, the fact that the exterior property photograph was taken in an unusual way leaks information that the vendor thinks there is something wrong with the house even though they never state what the problem is directly. Possibly the number of photos the vendor has supplied relative to the size of the property may be indicative. For a tiny property, there may be few areas to photograph but for a large house, few photos might be suspicious.

Machine learning can also be used to supply the features that form part of the hypothesis. Classification can be used on the property photos to pick out features before passing the result into a regression model. A classifier can detect what kind of room is featured in each of the supplied photos. Often house vendors are proud of the kitchen and keen to display it. If a photo of the kitchen is missing, that may indicate through its absence that the kitchen is in poor condition and needs to be replaced, which could be expensive and so perhaps the home value should be reduced proportionately.

Another example might be the price of an insurance quotation. Insurance companies have a lot of property information and might not be prepared to tell you directly what they know about an area. However the price of the quote relative to other similar properties nearby leaks information as to if there is something they know that you don't. An unusually high insurance quote on a specific property might be a red flag that would cause the value to be marked down.

There are lots of clever methods of obtaining input features by roundabout means. Economic activity in a country can be difficult to gauge because countries don't always publish reliable figures as they want to seem more prosperous than they actually are. Methods of obtaining more realistic numbers have included looking at the brightness of city lights at night on satellite photos. Countries that have more going on tend to have more light bulbs blazing. A particularly stark example is looking at the difference between North and South Korea at night. Looking at the amount of electricity being consumed is another useful metric that is correlated with how much industry is taking place.

Using someone else's model to influence your model can be a useful technique even if it is not understood how the model works. A machine learning system can learn how much weight it should apply to the output of another model even with no comprehension as to what it is doing, in effect it can learn how reliable another model is. Human models can also be fed in. For example, if financially viable, several local estate agents may be consulted for their estimates. A machine learning model can then be used to evaluate how reliable each of the agents is and how much weight to apply to each pricing estimate. One agent may need the business and have a propensity to overvalue properties to acquire custom while another agent might be inexperienced on the particular type of property and undervalue it. A model can learn how to weight the relevant inputs.

The factors that influence the price of a house may not all be to do with the property, many factors concern the situation of the potential buyers. The types of jobs available in the area and the pay levels of those jobs will affect house prices by placing a cap on what the locals can afford. Equally though, the relative willingness of outsiders to travel into the area is also important. If the area is a tourist hotspot it may be attractive for second home purchases and prices become relatively immune to the local economic situation. If there is a train line under construction to a major city, prices may be about to rise and the local economy should be given a low weight. When calculating future house prices, the drift in national trends could be important. If unemployment is generally rising then that might place an overall limitation on the rate at which properties increase in value.

Temporal information can be relevant. It may be imagined that the time of year influences the price that a home sells for. More house hunting may go on in the summer than the winter, driving up prices slightly through increased competition from buyers. Therefore if all of the pricing information is obtained only in a specific month, that could be a bias that causes error. The current date may also need to be supplied to the model as an input feature in order to provide the correct pricing information, so that it can adjust for seasonal variation.

Temporal information is important in recommendation engines for predicting user tastes. User interests tend to drift over time. The types of movies that you like now may not be the types of movies you liked even a few years ago. A user may have enjoyed superhero movies for a while but then tired of the genre and moved on to something else. A system that looks at the entire history of a user's movie choices might endlessly produce recommendations for superhero movies because the user had watched a lot of them previously, but fails to sufficiently weight the fact that the user has stopped watching the genre in recent times. The historical data in the model features might need to include the age of each of the user's selections as well as details about the movies such that the system can have the opportunity to give greater weight to more recent choices and less weight to older choices.

I have been an Amazon retail customer since the 1990s and Amazon retains my shopping history all the way back to the beginning. I wonder how much weight Amazon should apply to the CD purchases I made back then? Probably very little since I don't buy CDs any more and stream music online like everyone else. CDs are still very much available for sale but it would be a waste of a valuable advertising slot to recommend purchase. Technology has changed and it's no longer of interest. The first thing I bought on Amazon was a computer programming book, but again times have moved on and programming information is now mainly expected on the web.

Some trends might be static over time. A user that doesn't like sci-fi movies today probably won't like sci-fi movies in six months time either and so retaining a long history of previous selections is still important. Other trends might be periodic. A user might have a favourite movie that they watch repeatedly, but they probably don't want to watch it immediately again after they have just seen it. The system therefore might need to learn to leave a several month gap before suggesting a previously watched movie.

Failing to account for temporal information is a common fault in product recommendation systems. If a user has just purchased a washing machine, they probably don't want another one the following day as households normally only have one machine that lasts for several years. Using a scarce recommendation advertising slot to suggest purchase of a second washing machine is a wasted opportunity. The system needs to know the typical frequency with which users purchase different ranges of products, which could be discovered through data mining customer purchase records.

Movie selections are entirely related to the user's current mood which is unknowable to the machine learning system. The system might need to rotate through a number of varied choices in different genres that the user has previously watched rather than sticking to one specific tried and trusted genre. The user may normally watch dramas and these appear frequently in the movie viewing history, but this evening they want something different and are in the mood for a comedy. The system can't really know that, the only information it has is the history of movies viewed and so is most likely to present another drama. One way to solve this is with segmentation of choices. For example the system is trained to produce outputs in different genres and several genre options are presented to the user simultaneously. It may generate three dramas, three comedies, three fantasy movies and three mysteries. The user then chooses from the genre range that best matches their mood in the moment.

A problem with segmentation is that it can go too far. Almost all users likely have an attention span limit for scrolling through lists of genres and might give up if too many options are presented. There is a well researched phenomenon called "the paradox of choice" where too much choice can cause anxiety and the user gives up due to being overwhelmed or through lack of energy. Findings regarding the validity of this problem are mixed, but some sub-groups of users may be predisposed to it. For certain users the system may do better by being more of a dictator and suggesting that they are getting either movie A or B and that's the choices on offer. This is somewhat similar to the situation that sometimes happens with linear broadcast television, where the viewer would just switch on and watch whatever happened to be on the screen at the time. It's too much effort to trawl the 1000+ satellite channels (content segmentations) that may or may not have something of interest. Sometimes having the responsibility for choice limited is actually welcomed by users.

Offering a binary choice and nothing else may be a somewhat extreme user interface, but the system could offer a "more" button to receive additional movie suggestions. The system might tailor how many choices are presented to the user at once on each click of the button depending on their propensity to just select whatever it presents on the first try or whether they repeatedly click the button.

Another method of solving the mood problem is to provide features that allow the user to select the genres of current interest and directly inform the system. The user's specified choices are then used as a strong feature in the selection algorithm. However, this may be less successful as it introduces "friction" into the user interface. That is, the more effort you require from the user, the less likely they are to use the system. Surprisingly small amounts of required effort can turn users away. Who feels like filling in a preferences survey when slumped on the sofa looking for entertainment?

A variation on this is to allow the user to easily vote on choices the algorithm puts before them. It shows the user a popular drama and they downvote it, therefore that's an input feature to the system to reduce the probability of a drama as the next choice. Information about where the user has recently been in the movie selection application can also be used as a feature. For example if the user has been browsing around the comedy section but selected nothing, that might be a signal the machine learning system can use to bump the probability of outputting a comedy.

A small degree of randomness can be useful. For example the system might try to occasionally suggest a generally popular movie selected at random that is not within the genres the user normally watches. The system might hit on a new genre that the user didn't know they liked and widen the field of possible choices. This is described as breaking out of a "local minima", which is a specific region of the possible space of choices that the user gets stuck in because they don't know about what else exists. The user might be quite content in their valley, but occasionally the system needs to show them what is over the mountains in case that turns out to be better.

Randomness will likely be injected as a special programmed case and not directly as an input feature as the system won't learn much from a random number. A recommendation system might produce several output movies with a probability that it thinks the user could like the movie. The way the system would work normally is it would sort the probabilities in descending order and pick movies from the top of the list with the highest probability that the user may enjoy the content. The system may be programmed such that at random it ignores the high probability predictions and selects a movie from lower down the list that is well outside of the range of probabilities it would normally choose. Perhaps it occasionally selects a movie with only a 30% chance the user will enjoy it.

Random factors are often described as "creativity" in systems. There's a fine balance because the system can't be too random otherwise the user will perceive that it is ignoring their preferences. Randomness is an important feature for content generation systems such that they do not produce the same content each time from the same inputs. A system might ratchet up the creativity setting if the user continuously declines the movies it is selecting (more frequently pick low probability movies).

Sophisticated recommendation systems also learn to modify how they present content and tailor it to the user. For example a movie recommendation system may have several thumbnail images available for each title. One thumbnail might show a close-up of a lead actor in the film, another might place emphasis on the action in the movie. The user's reaction to the same movie can be different depending on exactly how the movie is promoted. A movie with a presentation concentrating on storyline might cause the user to pass, but with an emphasis on the action present in the film, they might be inclined to watch it. Similarly if the user has watched several movies with the lead actor, then a thumbnail specifically depicting that actor might best attract their attention.

It's important not to allow a system to mislead when granting the capability to modify the presentation of content and to make sure that the depiction of the movie is representative of what it really contains. Spam news articles routinely use a photo of a celebrity to attract attention and then the content the user is actually presented with contains no information about the person depicted. Misrepresentation, even if accidental, will very rapidly cause the user to become jaded and ignore the system or go elsewhere. Recommendation systems will quite happily learn to lie as that produces the best short term outcome to maximise user engagement with the system. It's just doing exactly what it has been told to. The system is oblivious to the long term business damage from loss of reputation.

A machine learning system needs feedback such that the system performance can be evaluated. Is it a good machine learning system or a poor one? In the case of the house price guesser, the feedback mechanism is quite straightforward. The price differential between the price it guessed and the price the property sold for is measured and it aims to minimise the difference. In the case of the recommendation system though, it can be a little more complex to define what success means. Is success maximising the number of movies the user views? Is it perhaps total minutes of video watched? Is it perhaps related to the number of movies the recommendation system has to present to the user before they select something? The fewer movies it produces before persuading the user to watch something, the greater the success of the system.

The success factor influences what the system will ultimately do. For example if its aim is to get the user to watch the most minutes possible, then it may start recommending longer movies or the extended director's cut above everything else. If the metric it is being measured on is most movies watched then it might go completely in the opposite direction and recommend the shortest movies it can to persuade the user to rattle through as many distinct titles as possible. Neither of these directions might produce the greatest customer satisfaction. There might be a better metric that defines what best serving the user actually means.

Features that are available might not always be easily perceivable to a human. A specialist sensor might greatly reduce the complexity of a robot machine learning system, dramatically simplifying the inputs. As mentioned previously, robots used for sorting objects often use multi-spectral imaging cameras able to see in varying wavelengths which reduces the complexity of the identification of plastics that reflect different bands of the electromagnetic spectrum.

Robots that need to navigate often make use of range finding systems. These might be ultrasonic sensors that work like sonar, bouncing a sound signal off potential obstacles ahead, but more recently laser based systems have come to the fore which are more precise. LIDAR (Light Detection and Ranging) is a form of range finder that is often used in robotics that can calculate the precise distance to an object but also has the advantage of being able to define the exact point in space where the range measurement has been taken. This yields an improvement over ultrasonic measurements that are much more diffuse and can't easily differentiate between multiple objects. A robot vacuum cleaner using an ultrasonic sensor to detect obstacles might have a good idea that there is a wall ahead but fails to notice a wine bottle on the floor just in front of the wall as it doesn't have the resolution to differentiate the two objects. That red wine will never come out of the carpet. LIDAR can however provide a much more detailed picture of the distances to all objects within its field of view and can see there is a small object just in front of the wall, potentially avoiding it.

There has been debate in self-driving cars as to whether a vehicle needs only cameras or should also have a LIDAR system. The problem with LIDARs is that they are an added expense and high resolution cameras, through the commoditisation effects of mobile phones, have now become negligibly cheap. Most LIDARs have not been commoditised in the same way as they haven't to date had mass market uses.[2] People drive a car using only their eyes and, so the theory goes, a set of cameras able to observe different directions should be able to do the job equally as well. It is possible, but quite difficult, to accurately calculate ranges to obstacles from a camera and LIDARs provide a short-cut to the problem that is centimetre accurate.

LIDARs are very precise with fine-grain resolution but have the disadvantage of being disrupted by bad weather. Rain and fog can interfere with LIDAR measurements. Radio based radar is immune to the weather issue but lacks fine resolution, somewhat like ultrasonic sensors, and can only really tell there is a large obstacle ahead but not as easily define the shape of it and cannot see some obstacles that do not reflect the radio signal. Radar will see a truck but might miss a bollard.

Cameras have an advantage that they can classify objects using colour information that a LIDAR can't see (it can only detect distances). For example a camera can tell there might be a cyclist ahead even if it doesn't correctly estimate the distance. A LIDAR may only see a bunch of blobs at a specific distance. By classifying the type of object the future motion of the object can be better predicted.

---

2   One system did have a mass market use in the form of the Microsoft Kinect, became inexpensive and was regularly used in robotics research.

The technologies have differing advantages and disadvantages and it would be helpful to use a different sensor in different circumstances. The outputs from multiple sensors can be fused together by an AI system which can learn how much to rely on the input from each device in different situations. If the LIDAR can see nothing of note but the radar says there's a large obstacle it can learn that the sensor takes precedence. If the camera is occluded it might give more weight to the LIDAR.

There are also mathematical techniques that can be used to combine the output of sensors with differing advantages to produce a unified output that is greater than any individual sensor alone. Navigation systems can often rely on multiple sensors with different limitations. There are several types of navigation satellites receivable by a mobile phone (not just GPS) that have varying capabilities and it is easy to lose the signal from some or all of them. Inertial sensors that measure acceleration can fill in gaps where satellite signals are unavailable but tend to suffer from drift where the sensor position starts to deviate from true after a while. A mathematical technique called a Kalman filter can be used to mix the strengths of each type of sensor and produce a single positional output that is better than any of the sensors individually.

Sensor input can quite significantly simplify a problem for AI and potentially make the solution much more reliable (or make the job possible in the first place). If you want to predict the health of crops, useful inputs might be soil moisture, temperature and pH sensors. Rough traffic volume present locally might be predicted by air quality, for which sensors are easily available. Popularity of a location might be predicted by activity on the bluetooth radio band as many people carry a phone.

Selecting the features that go into the AI system isn't really a stage in the development of a system that is exclusive to programmers. It should involve many people with business knowledge, domain knowledge, user opinions and the widest diversity of views. This is a stage in the system development for brainstorming and where maximum creativity is needed. The coders and mathematicians can then work with ideas generated to find out what is actually true statistically and that becomes the input features to the AI system.

Image Generation

Image generation was one of the earliest forms of generative AI that caught public attention. In current incarnations a text prompt can be entered and the machine attempts to produce an often very realistic image that represents what was requested. Demonstrations of the systems routinely use fanciful examples that are less likely to exist as real photos to emphasise the fact that the resulting image is artificial. An example that somehow became the go-to "hello world", or first test prompt to use when learning the technology, is to ask for a picture of an astronaut riding a horse. There is no generative image system worth its salt that cannot produce a photo of an astronaut on a horse (see Figure 14).

Image generation is now everywhere with dozens of websites, both free and commercial, that are able to produce artificial photos on demand. The technology has found its way into image manipulation software and image generation is now offered on popular search engines as an alternative to image search. There are also open source implementations that are largely as good as the commercial versions.

Figure 14 - The image generation 'hello world' prompt- an astronaut riding a horse

While the technique had been around years earlier, the first model to popularise the technology was nVidia StyleGAN released in 2018. The "GAN" portion of the name stands for Generative Adversarial Network and is a general term for a particular form of neural network training. StyleGAN is better known as "this person does not exist", named after a 3rd party website that was created to make the technology more accessible to the public. Many similar clone websites soon appeared.

StyleGAN could only produce images of arbitrary faces. It could not be directed by a prompt and only random faces could be generated. However, the photographic realism of the images that were produced startled many as the level of fidelity was not something that had been seen previously and StyleGAN was widely praised in the popular media.

StyleGAN was released publicly as open source and researchers quickly took hold of it. Variations appeared that could be partially directed by the user to produce faces with particular characteristics.

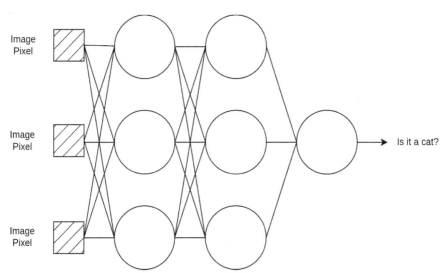

Figure 15 - A simplified model of an image classifier with three image pixel inputs to the left and classification output to the right

The way these networks produce images is somewhat like a neural network classifier but running in reverse. Imagine a classifier is built that can identify cats. There will be an input layer that takes in the pixels of the image of a cat and an output neuron (see Figure 15). The output neuron might register with a value nearer 1 when the input pixels look like a cat and a value nearer zero when the image is not a cat.

What would happen though if we wired up the classifier structure backwards (see Figure 16)? That is, you turn the "is a cat" output into an input and feed in a '1' then work backwards tracing your way from the output neuron all the way back to the input pixels?

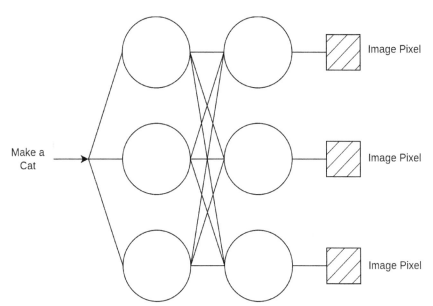

Figure 16 - The classifier reversed, an image generator network

Well it turns out, with appropriate training, you can get a picture that looks something like a cat out the other end. This classifier wired up backwards arrangement is known as a "generator" network. Instead of having a single "is a cat" input though, the generator typically has multiple inputs (see Figure 17). The meaning of what these inputs do is not easily understood but they all mean "is a cat" in a subtly different way. Perhaps one input has some influence on the colour of fur and another input has some impact on the length of the tail. The correspondence between the inputs and the image produced is unlikely to be straightforward though.

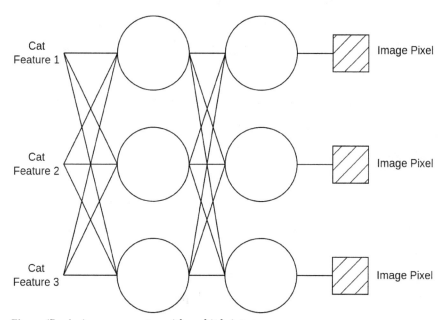

Figure 17 - An image generator with multiple inputs

With several inputs, there are a lot of possible combinations of those inputs. It turns out if you feed in varying combinations into the inputs then you get pictures of different cats out. Exactly what kind of picture you receive is difficult to control but if you feed in identical inputs you get exactly the same picture of a cat every time. The set of values that are fed into the generator inputs is called the "seed".

The generator neural network has a natural tendency to self-organise. Say you play around with the inputs at random and by chance find a combination that generates a short-haired grey cat. If you vary the input values only very slightly from that position, it will produce a different short-haired grey cat that looks somewhat like the first one. If the inputs are again randomised to something completely different it might come up with a white floof sat in a Bond villain's lap. Just very slightly varying the inputs from those settings will come up with other similar moggies befitting Dr Evil. Similar characteristics in the output images tend to be found around the same areas in the space of possible input values. Cats that are dissimilar require inputs that are far apart and producing cats that are very similar requires inputs that are virtually identical on each occasion.

The set of all possible combinations of inputs to the neural network is known as the "latent space". This idea of specific positions in the latent space representing particular features in the output image is an important concept that will be heavily relied on.

To train the generator network though, we need to add another element to the story. The generator network is paired up with a further component, the second part being the "adversary" or "discriminator" network. A classifier is structured in a conventional manner, like that in Figure 15, which is intended to be a cat detector. The generator network is then chained into the cat detecting classifier such that the output image from the generator is feeding directly into the classifier image input (see Figure 18). This pairing of a generator network and adversary is where the term Generative Adversarial Network (GAN) originates from.

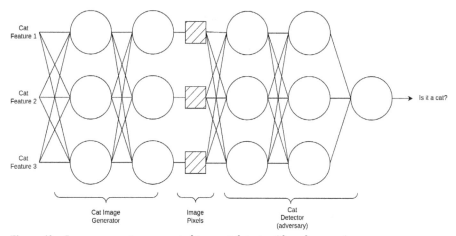

Figure 18 - Image generator connected to a cat detector (the adversary)

A random selection of values are fed into the cat generator inputs. Somewhere in the middle a cat picture is produced, but it won't be a very good cat picture to begin with, in fact probably quite terrible. The cat detector then receives the image and declares it a failure. However, the cat detector produces a value indicating exactly how cat-like the image is. Some attempts at producing a cat will be just very slightly better than others by chance and get fractionally higher scores. The cat generator is then trained with reference to the cat classifier output, using it as the "loss" value that influences the back-propagation adjustments to the network weights. The cat generator then very gradually gets better at producing images that are somewhat like a cat by effectively learning from what the cat detector knows about the problem. Eventually one image passes the cat detector and a cat generator is born.

Initially we don't make the cat detector particularly good to give the cat generator a chance. If we initially made the cat detector a highly discerning art critic, the generator would never persuade it to say any attempt it made was a cat and it wouldn't make any learning progress at all. At this stage the cat detector has accepted the cat generator's crayon stick figure, put it on the fridge and given the generator a pat on the head.

What incentive does the generator now have to produce better cats though? We need the generator to learn in incremental phases by ratcheting up the educational standard it needs to attain a little at a time to get it to improve the quality. What we can do is change the nature of the task slightly. We ask the classifier not just to determine if it is a picture of a cat, but detect if it is a genuine photo of a cat or one produced by the cat generator (a fake cat picture). The cat classifier is now more of a cat photo forgery detector.

The job of the cat generator is to get its fake cats into the "real cat" category and away from the forgeries category. Quite sneakily though, every time the cat generator manages to slide a forgery past the cat detector, the detector is re-trained a little more to differentiate real cat photos from the forgeries and that specific example no longer works. The cat generator then has to get back to work again to improve the image quality in order to bypass the forgery detector. Every forgery the detector is trained on makes it better at understanding the cat forger's methods. The generator can do nothing but try and get better and better. Through this arms race, a very good cat generator is produced that can generate photorealistic images of cats (and the detector is discarded).

The rate of learning of the generator and the detector are managed to ensure neither gets too far ahead of the other in quality to ensure that the learning task remains possible. Ultimately though, the cat detection classifier might eventually plateau and just not be able to tell the difference any more no matter how much it is trained. At which point the GAN has gone as far as it can go.

It would be helpful if the process of cat generation could be directed, if we could tell the cat generator exactly what type of cat is wanted rather than have it produce random cats. Early attempts at this worked by using a machine learning system to try and locate a particular style of image in the latent space. A neural network would be shown a photo of a Bond villain cat, then it would adjust the inputs to the generator network until it managed to determine the appropriate input values that caused an image to be generated that closely matched the image it has been shown. A note could then be made of where the relevant position is in the latent space and variations on that type of cat could be generated for ever more.

Using latent search can enable some nifty effects. For example if you find the grey cat in the search space and find the white cat in the search space then you can morph one into the other. Starting with the input values that produce the grey cat you gradually move in the direction of the inputs that represent the white cat. Then one image tends towards the other and images of all the kinds of cats that are somewhere in between the grey and white ones can be generated. The morph is not usually smooth and aspects of the cat and background will change rapidly and unpredictably, but a gradual transition in cat characteristics from one to the other can normally be seen.

This technique can also be used to perform a kind of image manipulation. One such effect is changing the expression on the face in a photo. A face might be generated by a GAN but it doesn't have the desired expression, perhaps the face is frowning and we want a photo of a smiling face. If the position in the latent space is identified where images with a smiling expression are generally located, then we can slowly move in that direction and the image we originally generated will tend towards a smiling expression.

When the generator self-organises, as in the StyleGAN approach, it places features in the latent space wherever it wants. This is somewhat like a photo library organised by a single librarian who has now retired with nothing written down about how the library works. The photos of short-haired grey cats are all together in a box somewhere and the photos of white floofs are all together in a box somewhere else. The organisation of the library is not random, some original thinking about the order in which the boxes ended up did occur, but no one is now quite sure what it is. We are left with the problem of checking all the boxes and then trying to write down where things happen to be. This involves a costly and involved search process. What would be much better is to impose a known system of organisation onto the photo library. Perhaps cat photos are arranged by breed, fur colour, size, age and other useful attributes. Then we can instantly know where the grey and white cats are located without the search process.

To apply a known ordering to the latent space an additional category label is passed along to both the generator and the detector. This is known as "conditioning". This might be in the form of an extra input that is 1 for grey fur and -1 for white fur. The detector now expects to have the relevant label when it makes its decision and the generator associates the label with what it is producing. This ends up having the effect of forcing the internal organisation of the generator to be split across this boundary and there is then a consistent input that can be applied to cause the generator to produce either grey or white cats.

The GAN interface style that is most popular with users is text to image. That is the user types in what they require as a text prompt, e.g. "Bond villain cat", and the system produces the relevant photo i.e. a grumpy looking white floof. This means the order that is imposed on the latent space needs to relate to the English language and all of the quirks that come with that.

Methods are available to convert English sentences (or any other language) into a list of numbers that encode meaning. These methods will be covered in the following large language model chapter where the same techniques are used. When two English sentences are typed with similar meaning, the numbers that are produced are in the same area. When two sentences with dissimilar meanings are entered, the numbers end up far apart. This is essentially another latent space but for words instead of images. The set of numbers can be applied as the conditioning factor to the generator and discriminator, just like the cat fur colour parameter. This causes the image latent space to be organised according to the meaning of language. From this arises a system that can generate images from text. Rather than just randomly stumbling about the latent space and seeing what we can find, now we know exactly where to look in the latent space to find images that represent the meaning of words. Now we have a system with the very powerful capability to generate images from text "prompts".

Image generation systems may offer some features to assist the machine with understanding the text, which it is not always adept at. It will usually understand the words but not necessarily exactly how the words relate to each other, especially if those relationships are complex. The user might type in "Grey cat but not fluffy" and the system has trouble understanding the negative and generates fluffy cats. For this reason it is usually possible to provide the system with at least some basic assistance in comprehending the grammar. It is almost always possible to specify if words should apply in a positive or negative manner i.e. the prompt may be rephrased as a positive prompt "grey cat" and a negative prompt "fluffy". Most GAN models can also apply relevance weightings to the words in the prompt i.e. how much attention the system should be placing on each word. Some GANs can accept artistic styles such as "cartoon" or "oil painting".

Sometimes it is difficult to describe what is required in words but fairly easy to explain it in pictures. Say for example a picture of a house is required. The GAN will be able to generate an image of an arbitrary house very easily from a text description, but when a specific house is wanted it's difficult to come up with the exact words to persuade the system to do as required. For example, consider this prompt:

"Very small house, oriented at 45 degrees to the camera with the front facing the camera and an open porch area. The porch has a pitched roof as does the main house."

Figure 19 - An image of a house generated to the text specification but it is difficult to describe in words exactly the image that is required

The system does come up with something that technically matches the description (see Figure 19) but frustratingly does not produce exactly what was imagined. A lot of non-obvious wordsmithing is required to get an exact match for the image that is in your head. To solve this problem, variations of GANs exist that can accept an image as input in addition to a text prompt. One picture is worth 1000 words. The user can supply a fairly crude drawing of what it is they require and then provide some words to describe it. For example the user may draw a picture of a house (see Figure 20), which need not have too much artistic merit, then supply a text prompt of "house photo" and the system is able to combine the two prompts into a photorealistic image that looks somewhat like the supplied sketch (see Figure 21).

Figure 20 - Sketch of a house usage as an input to influence the image generator

Figure 21 - Resulting house image described by a combination of an input sketch and also a text description

The way this is working is the input to the generator has not just been conditioned on text but also conditioned on images. An additional neural network is placed on the front of the generator that can compress an input image down into a latent space (like the generator in reverse). This latent space is then an additional conditioning variable (library organisation) to the generator. Some special training data may also have been used to improve the performance in certain special circumstances e.g. sketches that have been paired up with photos. These pairings can be produced by using a conventional edge detection filter on a photograph which produces a line drawing style result.

Sometimes an image is generated that is nearly what is required but is not quite right. There are solutions to this such as "inpainting". This is where a region of an image can be highlighted (usually by painting on the image with a brush tool), a text prompt supplied and then the system can replace the highlighted region with the object described by the text prompt whilst retaining and working around the rest of the image. So it allows a generated image that is nearly correct to be modified to perfect it. This is essentially automated photo editing. A GAN generated image of a cat is shown below (see Figure 22).

Figure 22 - GAN generated image of a cat

By use of inpainting, the same cat can be generated but with a hat (see Figure 23).

Figure 23 - Image modified using an inpainting technique to add a hat on the cat

The image can be amended any number of times. Now a jacket is added to the above image using further inpainting (see Figure 24).

Figure 24 - Additional inpainting performed to add a jacket to the previously inpainted GAN image

The same technique can be used on real photos and the original image does not have to be GAN generated. So if you're having trouble getting a hat onto Bitey McClaws for that perfect photo and do not have any image editing skills, inpainting is the answer.

A related effect is "outpainting". This allows an image to be extended. An existing photo can be supplied and the system will try and imagine what may be to the left, right, above or below. It is a little known fact that Leonardo da Vinci originally painted the Mona Lisa in widescreen. It was terrible of the Louvre to crop it like that. Below is the rarely seen right hand half (see Figure 25).

Figure 25 - The left hand section of the image is (part of) the original Mona Lisa. The right hand side of the image is fictitious and was generated by a GAN using outpainting to match the style of the original work.

Outpainting guesses at what might have been present in the photo based on training data for similar images. It is not possible for the system to produce an accurate depiction of what was really there, just a plausible reimagination of it. However, if other photos of the same scene are available it is possible to use them as references for outpainting which improves the guesswork and the system can produce something closer to a depiction of the real image subject. For example if another historic painting were available of roughly the same location as the Mona Lisa, it would be possible to use that as a reference image for a more accurate result.

CycleGANs are a method of modifying the style of an image and can be useful for many advanced image manipulation effects. The technique learns what is common about a group of training examples and then applies that common factor to an input image. Examples are turning a photo of a daytime scene into night, converting a photo of a horse into a zebra or changing the artistic style of an image, such as converting a photo into a cartoon. Inpainting is a generalised tool but CycleGANs focus on performing one very specific image effect. CycleGANs pay close attention to the input image and carefully use it as a reference to guide what it outputs such that the essential characteristic of the original photo is retained. Inpainting by contrast generates an entirely new object and then figures out how to imperceptibly photoshop it into the image. CycleGANs are more about translating the image from one form to another. It's somewhat like language translation but for images, it's converting the visual style inherent in the images from one form to another.

CycleGANs are probably at the heart of many novelty photo manipulation mobile phone apps, although since the source code is usually proprietary it is unclear if this assertion is correct. The image manipulation performed by apps is often described as a "filter" in consumer language although the techniques are not mathematical filters in the classical sense, they are almost certainly a neural network technique.

If we consider the challenge of producing a system to convert photos of horses into zebras, it would be a near impossible task to somehow obtain thousands of photos of horses and zebras in precisely the same pose where the animals looked similar and were against the same background. CycleGANs have the useful property that they do not require precisely paired-up training examples. All that is required is arbitrary photos of any horses and any zebras and the photos can be quite different. The system then learns the characteristics of each subject and how to apply the characteristics of one animal to the other.

These systems work by using a pair of image-to-image GANs. One is to be trained to convert horses to zebras, but the other one is trained to convert zebras back to horses. The trick is the two GANs are evaluated on how well the pair can recover the original image by passing the image from one to the other. A horse photo is input and converted to a zebra by the first GAN, then converted back to a horse again by the second GAN. The discrepancy between the double converted photo and the original photo of a horse is then compared and the GAN loss is calculated from this. This is like converting English to French, then converting back to English again and checking you got exactly the same sentence. The more different words appear in the double converted phrase compared with the original English then the larger the loss.

A check is put in the middle of the two GANs, which is a high quality zebra detector. This prevents the GANs from cheating and just passing the original image of a horse straight through without any modification. The quality of the zebra produced is also passed into the training loss (see Figure 26).

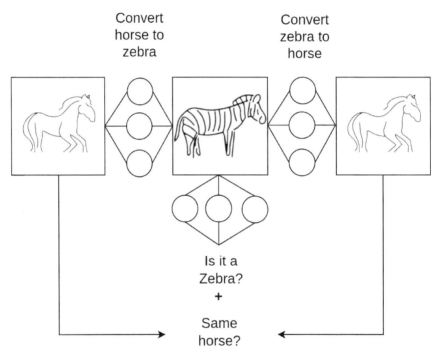

Figure 26 - Diagram of how a CycleGAN works.

The fact that the CycleGAN has to be able to reconstruct the identical original horse image pixel for pixel makes sure that it stays as close as possible to what the original horse looked like and doesn't just try and generate a brand new arbitrary zebra, because it has to be able to recover the original horse pose and the background the horse was against. So it passes through as much information as it possibly can from the original photo and then just applies the minimum amount of zebra features to pass the zebra checker. So the best thing it can do to keep everything in balance is paint some stripes on the original horse photo.

Large Language Models

Large Language Models (LLMs) are generative AI systems that can understand natural language input (text written by people) and/or produce text output which resembles that written by a person. In this case "large" is a reference to either the fact that the system has seen a lot of training data or that the number of neurons in the model is significant compared with previous models or both. The exact definition of large will probably drift over time and the LLMs of today will quickly seem quite small by comparison with those available in the future.

LLMs were popularised by the appearance of ChatGPT from OpenAI in 2022, although the concept had been around previously and other products were already available. On release, ChatGPT rapidly caught the imagination of the public, acquired more than 100 million users and received widespread acclaim. It was the first good quality implementation of sufficient scale to showcase the LLM as a generalised tool with many practical applications.

The vast number of uses to which the ChatGPT model could be applied and the unprecedented degree to which the public embraced the technology surprised many in the industry. This triggered an explosion in research with a collection of other companies (including other major tech companies) releasing competing services in short order, some with a degree of panic about losing market share. Within only a few months ChatGPT was just one of many high quality LLMs available, but at the time of writing remains the best known brand.

ChatGPT has found applications in question answering, summarisation, writing fiction, generating business ideas, writing song lyrics, translation and is particularly strong in assisting with software development. Many users though have simply found it entertaining, since it delivers the novelty of a machine genuinely capable of holding a convincing in-depth conversation, a task that preceding AI systems had not been particularly adept at. Many previous AI systems have variously claimed to pass the "Turing Test", that is write text that is indistinguishable from what a human may write, but ChatGPT is probably the first publicly available system that could genuinely lay claim to that crown without any caveats being applied.

The majority of LLMs currently available are neural network based and work by performing text "completions". A completion is the capability to predict what the next word in a sentence may be based on previous words and is a variation of a sequence prediction style AI task. The concept is very similar to what a smartphone touchscreen keyboard does. A virtual on-screen keyboard lacks tactile feedback and is not as easy to type on as a large physical keyboard composed of real switches, so it tries to help by reducing the amount of typing necessary. When a user types on a software keyboard it probabilistically suggests what it thinks the next word to be typed may be (see Figure 27).

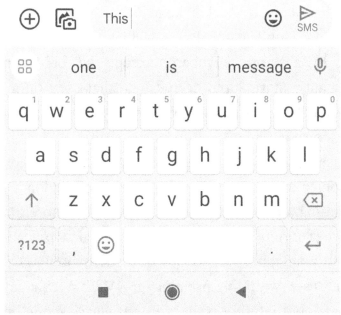

Figure 27 - Mobile phone predictive text software keyboard

Usually the keyboard user only occasionally picks a machine generated suggestion, however imagine if every suggestion made by the phone were selected continuously and the human user typed nothing at all. The phone would produce a full English sentence and usually the sentence produced would make grammatical sense and be valid in terms of the language generated. While these keyboards are improving, normally the sentence generated is not appropriate to the context of what may be required. It may be grammatically correct language but isn't a very useful sentence and the meaning is not always what the user intends to write.

The process by which large language models work is essentially identical to always picking the next suggestion made by a phone keyboard, except the LLM model is significantly more sophisticated than that used on a phone and is much more likely to suggest words that are appropriate to the context.

Language models (without the "large" prefix) are not a new phenomenon and have been a novelty entertaining people (or causing a nuisance) for some 40 years or more. Posts on Usenet (a forum system on the internet that preceded the web) were infamously made using language models. One fake Usenet user with the pseudonym "Mark V. Shaney" was making robot internet posts with a language model in 1984. The name of the user is intended to give a cryptic clue to computer scientists that the user is a robot and not a real person. The name is a variation of the term "Markov chain".

A Markov chain is formed by constructing a graph of words (see Figure 28). A graph in this sense is not meaning a chart (as may be produced by a spreadsheet) but the mathematical sense of the term, where a series of nodes are connected by links. Markov chains themselves are a very old mathematical idea, with the first paper being published by Andrey Markov in 1906.

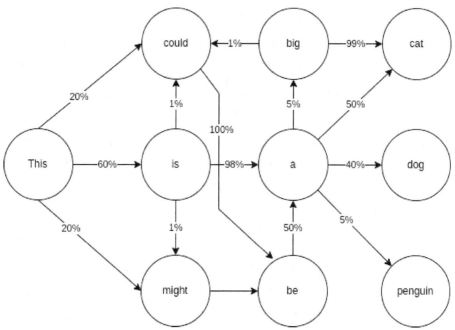

Figure 28 - A Markov chain shown as a graph

Each word is represented by a node and the links all have a probability on them. We begin with a word selected at random somewhere in the graph, it doesn't matter where, then roll some dice and move to a new node in the graph. Links with a high probability are more likely to be followed based on the dice roll. Links with a low probability are less likely to be followed, but might sometimes be followed. As nodes are passed through, a sentence is formed. The probabilities are produced by inspecting a large amount of text and calculating the frequency with which one word normally follows another.

Markov chains have limitations because they don't naturally record much of the history of the previous words spoken. The next word really only depends on the current position (word) in the graph and the system has no real clue what it said just a few words previously. This is different to the way a person speaks, where we can (usually) remember what we just said and that memory has an impact on what is said next. Markov chains can produce valid text that is sometimes convincing (especially if people are unaware they are talking to a robot and are prepared to give the benefit of the doubt). The technique though quickly hits a brick wall and not much progress in text quality can be made.

The neural networks in large language models are producing a result somewhat like a Markov chain but internally operate in a quite different and much more sophisticated way. The LLM systems produce one word at a time, just like a Markov chain. A neuron in the network could possibly be representing a single word like a node in a

Markov chain, but more usually each neuron is representing a much more nuanced fractional contribution to an abstract concept. There is far from an exact one-to-one correspondence between neurons in an LLM and words. Parts of the model also have an informational processing role that prepares the language in a way that is easier for the model to deal with. It's a considerably more complex picture that is much more difficult to visually interpret with a graph. In truth, AI researchers don't really understand exactly what the LLMs are doing at a granular level and they are very challenging and time consuming to analyse. It is very difficult to point at one specific neuron and assert it has a particular job or articulate what that job may be.

Unlike the Markov chain, the large language model is provided with a sense of history of what has been said previously. It can usually recall up to several thousand words of text prior to what it is about to say. This vastly improves the quality of the output over a Markov chain as this history has a strong impact on the next word to be produced.

The vast size of the modern LLM neural network (with often hundreds of billions of connections) enables it to have an intrinsic internal memory of a huge array of concepts, that is information encoded within the structure of the nodes and the weights on the links between them. LLMs are trained on vast amounts of text, usually equating to a substantial fraction of the text available on the publicly accessible web. Markov chains were often historically implemented on comparatively tiny computer systems and lacked the depth of the modern LLMs.

Modern LLMs have many capabilities from answering questions to writing software. All the LLM is doing though is predicting what the next word in a sentence may be and everything it does is a variation of this process. It can be difficult to understand how these more complex behaviours may arise but it is really a function of the scale of training data it has seen.

When a question is asked on the web, it may often be immediately followed by an answer. On a web forum, a page usually starts with a question and then the next text found on the page is answers, or at least attempts at answers. An answer immediately following a question is a much more common outcome than a sudden change in topic to something unrelated. Whatever the user of the LLM system types in is placed into the history of the previous conversation that the neural network has access to. So if the user types in a question, the LLM system is effectively informed it has just generated the question text and that history biases what it will say next. Given an answer to the question is the next most probable text to be found in the training data that was used to produce the LLM in the first place, an answer is most likely what the LLM will attempt to produce next. It is simply mirroring the probabilities of word sequences seen on the internet. This is how a text completion system can naturally acquire the property of being a question answering system simply through the volume of text it is trained on.

There are many wrong answers to questions on the web and so the LLM system in correspondence has some probability of generating a wrong answer as well. However, common questions have more right answers and fewer wrong answers. Therefore, the system training should assign a higher probability to the words comprising the right answer. It is really using the "wisdom of crowds" effect to hopefully produce the correct results.

There is of course some risk that the most frequent answer on the web is in fact wrong, perhaps due to popular misconceptions or cultural biases, but more often than not a right answer most frequently follows a question. An LLM is more likely to generate wrong answers for obscure questions as there are fewer examples in the training data and it is more likely to be overcome with noise and misinformation.

A common convention is for an LLM to have a setting called "temperature". This setting may be hidden on popular chatbots and public facing user interfaces to LLMs found on the web, but is usually made available to programmers. This setting biases the LLM to only following paths that have either a high or low probability. When producing a question answering system, a low temperature setting is normally used. This causes the LLM to be more likely to generate the highest probability text next, which in the case of questions and answers will be the most frequently occurring answer to the question on the web. This is hopefully, but not guaranteed to be, the correct answer.

A low temperature setting, however, has the side effect of causing the LLM to say the same thing every time. If a user wants the LLM to generate fiction, they may not be satisfied that it always produces the same fiction on every single occasion. In this scenario a high temperature setting is used. This causes the LLM to follow less probable paths. The temperature setting is sometimes referred to as a "creativity" setting as it causes the LLM to come out with somewhat left-field answers and make more illogical jumps.

LLMs are not good at everything, they are notoriously terrible at maths, just like the average person from whom they are trained. There is a certain irony that the LLM is being executed on a machine that can flawlessly perform up to trillions of calculations per second with absolute precision but yet gives completely the wrong answer to a simple addition. The solution to this problem that is now being used is to try and detect when the LLM is being asked a maths question and pass it on to a regular calculator instead. The LLM responds with English language but inserts a template and a calculator fills in the answer e.g. the LLM might respond with:

The answer to 27 plus 36 is {27+36}

A conventional calculator program subsequently scans the LLM output and detects the template in braces, which is requesting a calculation to be performed, computes the answer and replaces the template with 63 before the response is presented to the user.

There are doubtless many more questions that are better answered with conventional computing, such as questions with very specific factual answers like "what is the population of London?" The LLM might detect a question that it can answer using reference material, but not directly supply the answer from the LLM itself. Instead it would produce a template stating that a factual answer was needed and compute the response from a database of authoritative and fact-checked information.

The population of London is {population,London}.

This template method cures the issue of the probabilistic gamble where the LLM will sometimes produce wrong answers for straightforward questions. The LLM of the future will play to its strength of producing the natural language part of the answer and work in tandem with conventional computing to complete the solution.

Neural networks only deal in numbers, so getting words into one presents an immediate challenge. The solution that is used is to assign a numerical value to each word in the dictionary. For example:

...

A = 1

Aardvark = 2

About = 3

Accent = 4

...

The neural network is then able to deal with the words using the corresponding enumeration. One problem with this approach is handling words that do not appear in the dictionary. What about foreign names or specialist technical terms or fictional words? For these words, they can be built out of other words that we already have in the dictionary. For example, if we did not have "authorship" in the specific dictionary we used, it can be encoded as two words "author" and "ship" that we do have in the dictionary. For words where we do not have any appropriate subset words occurring in English, we can add additional non-English strings of characters to the dictionary to cover all eventualities. In fact we include all 26 individual letters in the dictionary as pseudo words, so if it comes down to it, we can just encode a word as a list of the individual letters it contains. So we might have a non-dictionary word like "tnetennba" encoded as t, net, en, n, ba.[3] This depends on

---

3   Good morning, that's a nice tnetennba.

what combinations of characters were available in the dictionary that was used.

As few strings as possible should be used to encode each word. When using commercial LLMs that are chargeable, it is common to find that usage is metered in "tokens". A token is usually left somewhat ill-defined by the LLM vendor but it refers to a sub-component part of a word. If the word occurs in the dictionary, then it may only be one token. If the word does not appear then it may be multiple tokens. Highly technical texts with uncommon words may need a lot of tokens whereas texts written in basic English may only need fewer tokens to encode the same length of text because the words appear in the LLM dictionary.

Dictionary order is not actually the optimum ordering for the words. We can get better performance out of the LLM by ordering words by their meaning instead, which is somewhat of a fuzzy concept with no specific obvious optimum ordering. Words might be grouped like this:

...

Tiger = 43

Wildcat = 44

Cat = 45

Moggy = 46

Kitten = 47

Whiskers = 48

Fur = 49

Dog = 50
Puppy = 51

...

Here all of the cat related words are pushed together and are numerically close to each other. The further away in concept or meaning the word is, the further away the number it is assigned. The word "toaster" will be numerically positioned a long way from cat, but the word "whiskers" is placed much nearer to cat in the ordering.

If the words are held in dictionary order, then it makes it harder for the LLM to reason about them. For example, if the LLM means to say "cat" but produces a number with just the tiniest of error, it turns into the next word in the dictionary which might be "cataclysm", a word with an entirely unrelated meaning. However, with words ordered by meaning, a slight error turns cat into moggy, which is still in the same area of meaning. Ordering by word meaning keeps the LLM thinking about cats instead of veering off into suddenly talking about disasters.

With a sorted list we have only one dimension to work with. We can go either up the list or down the list and that is all. However many words need grouping in multiple ways. For example puppy needs to be near dog and kitten needs to be near cat, but puppy also needs to be near kitten because they have related meaning in the sense of being a young animal. The problem with a simple list is we can't have it both ways and the words cannot be in multiple positions in the list. To solve this issue additional dimensions are introduced. So puppy can be located near dog along the Y dimension but also near kitten along the X dimension.

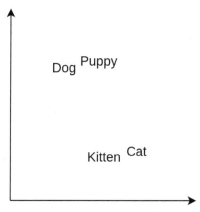

Figure 29 - Using multiple dimensions words can be adjacent along the different axes

LLMs currently in use often use a mind-bending 10,000 dimensions or more to represent words. It is near impossible to visualise 10,000 dimensional space but the system can handle this with no problem. So this means each word (or more specifically token) is input to the LLM as a list of 10,000 separate numerical values, or a "vector", and is known as an "embedding". What each of the dimensions in the vector actually means, who knows, but it's not really important as we can use the embeddings successfully with absolutely no clue what the dimensions mean. Construction of these 10,000 dimensional word lists would be a near impossible challenge by hand, so the task is itself performed using machine learning techniques. In the leading edge systems, billions of phrases scraped from the internet are examined to determine the best position in the dimensional space for each word based on the context in which it appears in the training data.

To construct sentences to feed into the LLM, the 10,000 number list is produced for each word successively in the input text (the prompt). These number lists then form the actual input to LLM. The output to the neural network is a similar number list. We do the reverse operation and look-up the word in the dictionary that the number list represents. That is, finally, how we get the next word in the completion. The completed word is then added to the history of what has been said so far by the LLM.

The completions process could go on forever, however it is expected that the LLM should, like a person, know when to stop talking i.e. it should know when it has provided a satisfactory answer. For this purpose there is usually a special word added to the dictionary called a "stop token". The LLM is trained to produce the special stop token at an appropriate juncture in the output that makes grammatical sense. The LLM is controlled by a software loop that tells it to keep cranking out words. The software watches for the appearance of this special stop token and when it sees it, it breaks out of the loop and stops asking the LLM to produce more text. It then reports the text produced thus far to the user as the answer to their query. When a programmer has low level control over the LLM it is usually possible to instruct the system to completely ignore the stop token and continue generating text up to a specific word limit that the programmer defines, however this limit might arise in the middle of a sentence and not be a natural grammatical stopping point for the text.

An enhancement that has been made to LLMs that has improved the quality significantly in recent years is called "attention". This is about adding context to words to resolve ambiguity and add additional meaning. For example, in the sentence "he took the cup from the shelf and filled it with coffee", what does the word "it" refer to? The word clearly refers to a cup. In the sentence "the tiger was seen in the bushes before it pounced on the prey", now the word "it" has something to do with tigers and nothing to do with coffee cups. However in both cases the word "it" gets the same embedding vector and therefore the neural network sees the word as having exactly the same meaning in both cases. The attention unit adds context to the word, either as being related to cup or tiger as appropriate. It does this by effectively creating a new word with no ambiguity, perhaps the new word is called "it-cup" or "it-tiger", and replaces the original word in the sentence. Now when the LLM sees this new contextualised word and is asked what word comes next, it's going to think more about coffee or tigers as appropriate and the generated text is more likely to be about the right context.

High quality LLMs currently cost a fortune to train, possibly in the millions of dollars at current public cloud prices. While it is quite realistic for an individual hobbyist or small company to build a language model, it will not be of the quality of such as ChatGPT due to this financial barrier. This cost will of course come down in the future, but it's not feasible right at the present time.

What can be done much less expensively however is take an existing model and specialise it. For example it is possible to take an existing model and add new training data to give the model the capability to talk about a new subject with which it is not familiar. Specialising an existing model benefits from all the hard work that has been done getting the model to understand language at all.

An alternative which is even easier is making use of the "context window". That is including a piece of text that you might like the model to talk about in the prompt. For example if the problem is to answer a question about a technical manual that the LLM has never seen, the content of the manual can be passed in together with a question asking the LLM to refer to the supplied text:

User: Can you tell me the size of disk the computer has in the following text:
<the full content of the manual is included here>

This approach works quite well. The difficulty is the context window has limitations. That is, the LLM can only process so much text at once. The context window size is largely a function of how much computational power is available and this is what causes the restriction. Context windows for LLMs are going up in size all the time. Typically context windows of a few thousand tokens are permitted for commercial offerings, but there are now LLMs that can work with book-length pieces of text that could feasibly accept a complete manual all at once.

The text to be worked with may just be too big though, perhaps we want to pass in a complete encyclopaedia that the LLM has never seen before. For this size of text even an LLM that can work with book-length chunks of text would be too small and it may be impractical to construct an LLM currently that can operate with a context window of this size. There are however tricks that can get around the problem.

One such trick is to use more conventional text processing to zone in on the right area of a text first. For example you could do a search on keywords within the text and then pull out possibly relevant paragraphs surrounding where the keywords are found. The paragraphs may or may not answer the question, many of them will be useless. The chunks of text can then be passed to an LLM to refine the answer. For example, all the paragraphs of text with matching keywords can be concatenated until they fill the LLM context window and then put into the prompt together with the question.

This trick has become known as Retrieval Augmented Generation (RAG) and is not just limited to single documents. It's slightly different to calling out to a database to directly answer a specific question using a template, such as "what's the capital of France", as shown previously. This approach combines a less capable conventional text retrieval database with the more capable language understanding of the LLM. The weaker database has the advantage of being able to hold vast amounts of information that the LLM couldn't possibly process within the context window e.g. maybe terabytes or petabytes of data. This kind of database can also produce answers in a fraction of a second, whereas the LLM is exceptionally resource intensive and could never inspect that amount of data in a reasonable time. The question is first asked of the less capable but larger database and it produces a wide scattering of paragraphs that might contain the answer, but it is not sure which paragraph actually answers the question because it just doesn't have the level of language understanding necessary to do that. The LLM puts the final brick in the wall by locating the right answer on behalf of the database within the subset of paragraphs selected.

Large language models can also be used to suggest actions as well as words. This can be done by training the model to output a particular token that can be easily detected by conventional software and interpreted. This is similar to the method used for solving the problem of accurate calculations. For example the language model may be trained to recognise actionable statements and output a machine detectable template.

> **User**: Hey Chatbot, can you make me a coffee?
> **LLM**: Sure, your coffee is brewing now
> {Action:CoffeeMachine=On}

When the template in braces is seen, conventional software converts it into a network request to remotely turn on the coffee machine. The LLM provides the useful service of understanding all of the dozens of variations of ways a user might ask for a coffee without each specific variation needing to be programmed.

The LLM can also use the template method to cause sequences of actions to be invoked and even refer back to itself. For example, the user may ask about recommended hotels but the LLM may not have any current information on the subject. What it can do is generate a sequence of steps, similar to a program, that can perform the function required and retrieve the information it needs to answer the question.

> **User**: Can you find me a hotel in Paris?
> **LLM**: Sure:

{WebSearch:"Paris hotel reviews"}

{VisitAndConcatenate:10}

{PromptLLM: "Using the following text generate a table of hotels, order by star rating with highest first: "+text}

The first template causes conventional software to perform a web search, which will return a selection of links to web pages based on the keywords "Paris hotel reviews". This will be a disparate collection of links that may or may not contain the required information. Some links might be spam and some might contain off-topic information, some might be news articles and others might be the lists of hotels that are needed. The second template causes the top ten links returned from the web search to be visited and the text presented on the pages extracted and concatenated. The third template causes the text to be passed back to the LLM in the context window and prefixed with a prompt. The prompt causes hotel details to be extracted and usefully organised into a tabular view by the LLM.

LLMs have proven to be generally good at programming. When trained with a large collection of source code they are able to produce at least modest snippets of software dozens of lines in length that are correct, directed by only an English description of what is to be done. For larger programs the current generation LLMS are less successful and tend to lack a sufficient context window and understanding of the goal, quickly wandering off-topic. However, production of short programs can be useful for control applications. For example if hundreds of examples of programs for how to control a robot in a domain specific language were available, an LLM can generalise from these to produce new programs. Say the following collection of example robot control programs is available for a coffee service robot:

1. Navigate from the first floor coffee shop to Bob's first floor office and present a coffee.
2. Navigate to the first floor lift and operate the doors
3. Navigate from the second floor lift to Alice's office

If Alice on the second floor asks for a coffee, there is no program that can deal with this situation and she will be out of luck. However a suitably trained LLM would be capable of merging together programs 2 and 3 to navigate to Alice's office, then extract the coffee presentation function from the 1st program. This kind of program merging is already routinely performed and LLMs are quite adept at generating new programs by recombining existing ones based on English instructions.

LLMs can also perform design work by constructing grammars that can then be interpreted by conventional software. The layout of a web page is described in language using the special grammar of HTML. There are instructions to place an image here and text over there and these instructions are interpreted as positions on a page where the elements go. Different grammars might be used for other layout and design problems. For example a grammar similar to HTML might be constructed for laying out a convention centre, with tokens suggesting where a particular stand and display feature might go. An LLM could then convert English instructions into a plausible layout for an event. Regular software would take the instructions and produce a diagram of the table layout in the room.

Another interesting approach is it is possible to persuade multiple LLMs to work cooperatively as teams. For example one LLM can be prompted that it has one particular team role and other LLMs can be prompted with different team roles with differing capabilities. The LLMs can then be connected together such that they have a conversation with each other without any human intervention with the goal of producing a product. The roles might be manager, web page designer and quality checker. The manager LLM instructs the two workers what shall be generated, the designer LLM produces output and the quality checker is tasked with finding defects in the work. The manager then coordinates between the producer and the quality checker. All three roles may in fact be the same LLM software, just with differing prompting. The LLM is continuously swapping hats and speaking as if it is in each of the roles.

We are only currently at the beginning of finding out what LLMs can do and there may be many interesting use cases that have not yet been discovered. LLMs haven't reached the peak of capability and even larger language models than exist today might be produced that are even smarter.

One curious limitation on the systems as they exist today might be the amount of text reasonably available for the LLMs to read. All humans combined just haven't written enough, or at least made enough text publicly available to advance LLM learning much further. The LLM companies have already acquired the most easily available portions of what there is to be found on the web. Companies that are gatekeepers to large troves of text are also realising the commercial value of the text to AI developers and are becoming less inclined to give access for free which may limit progress in the future. New n-shot methods of training might need to be developed to enable forward progress, where much less training data is used to deliver new LLM skills.

It seems likely that as the inference costs come down, LLMs will probably work their way into many more applications and become mixed with conventional software to fill in areas that are difficult to code. LLMs are already embedded into some word processors to make suggestions on writing, there are dozens of conversational chat apps and LLMs are now integrated into some programming tools. As LLMs speak a familiar language, more people are available to help with developing instructions and so more software may ultimately emerge.

Almost AI

The Mechanical Turk was a famous 1770 automaton that purported to be able to play chess. The machine consisted of a large box on which sat a chess board. Behind the board was a mannequin dressed in robes and a turban, at the time evoking the image of a sorcerer. The mannequin had moveable arms and could pick up and move chess pieces on the board.

The machine was very good at chess indeed, defeating some of the finest chess players in Europe. It was, however, a magic trick. A chess master was cleverly hidden inside a box under the machine who would operate it.

The constructor of the machine, Wolfgang von Kempelen, was not naive to the idea that deeply suspicious spectators would quickly want to know what exactly was in that particularly large person-sized box underneath the chess board. To deflect attention from the true means of operation, he installed a series of doors that could be opened to view the contents. Von Kempelen would go to great lengths to demonstrate that the box contained nothing but machinery. On opening the doors an onlooker would see only complex looking gear wheels. The wheels would move and the device would make noise when the Turk was "thinking". There was no human to be seen.

The essence of the trick was hiding the chess master from view. This was achieved by two main methods. Firstly, it was ensured only one of the doors was ever opened at once, this would enable the chess master to slide into the space that was not currently being inspected and cog wheels would slide across to replace him. This technique is now a staple of stage magic but may have been an innovation then, possibly being the first use of the trick. Secondly, the depth of the cabinet was deceptive and the machinery did not extend as far back as it appeared.

Von Kempelen would also employ various other illusionist misdirection techniques during games to keep the audience guessing. At one stage he kept a box on the desk surface that he would regularly inspect as if it somehow contained a secret or was essential to the operation of the device. The box had absolutely nothing to do with the operation of the Turk. Many people of the day speculated correctly as to the true nature of the machine but the secret was never formally revealed until after it was accidentally destroyed in 1854.

The Mechanical Turk was a machine purporting to be artificial intelligence but in fact was not. The concept hasn't gone away, there are examples of modern Turks, some of which are quite open about their operation but others more opaque.

Real Intelligence

Amazon has operated a platform, in fact called Mechanical Turk, for some years that enables work to be completed that would be difficult for a machine. The service farms the work out to people all over the world who complete it for a fee over the web. The humans are hidden in the process, but exist nonetheless and the end results just magically appear as if they may have been produced by a machine. Amazon is entirely open about the fact that real humans complete the work, it explains so clearly on the product page. The users of the service fully understand this too, in fact they expect the work to be completed by humans and that is the exact service they are paying for. However, it has not been unknown for "AI" companies to use humans behind the scenes in somewhat of a more obfuscated manner.

Some years ago one voice recognition company was suspected of this practice. The company offered transcription of voice messages for a per-message fee. Voice recognition technology was not at the time as advanced as it is today but the service offered by the company appeared to be unusually good. Researchers suspected that it might in fact be real humans doing the work. They tested their theory by comparing the performance of the system when transcribing different names. They sent themselves voice messages in English language containing names of varyingly difficult spelling with origins in different countries. It was found that the transcriptions of the names contained far fewer errors when the names were of Indian origin. This location was at the time a place where very low cost English speaking labour could be sourced. It may have been the case that the voice recognition was developed using training data with an origin in India, but that may be the generous interpretation. It was suspected the work was probably mostly being completed by a Mechanical Turk.

Social media companies have at various times made claims that their content moderation is performed using AI. However, often due to labour disputes, contractors have come to light in various countries that are conducting at least quite a lot of the moderation work. The presence of such large numbers of humans doing the work, who presumably cost quite a lot of money the company would rather not be paying, suggests that the automated moderation technologies may not be as advanced as may be implied.

If the job to be done is valuable, or the relevant company particularly well capitalised, there is always the possibility they may just be farming the work out to a low cost country and the AI may not be very effective. There's a risk that well funded AI start-up companies might be tempted to use the Mechanical Turk trick to cover for deficiencies in their technology. Problems arise if the company fails to ultimately produce functional AI, the capital runs out and they can no longer afford to employ humans.

AI that occasionally requires human intervention isn't necessarily a bad business model, in fact it can be a perfectly viable and sensible approach. The self-driving taxi companies are often employing humans to get the robots out of difficult situations the AI is unable to cope with. In effect they have figured out how to get one person to be able to drive more than one car at the same time. The risk to the business model is in the number of interventions that the employees need to make and the cost of the technology. If a human can on average drive four cars at once and the technology costs less than ¾ of a person, then a profitable gain can be made from using the AI system versus a fully occupied human driver. However, if humans need to intervene more often, then a loss will be made relative to just employing conventional taxi drivers to do the job full time.

Gamification

As with the production of training data, gamification has also been applied to difficult tasks to try and persuade humans to complete work in large numbers. This is essentially the Mechanical Turk approach but with a different human motivation. Usually the work is quite dull and humans are motivated by being paid to complete it, but in gamification it is attempted to make the work fun or intellectually stimulating by converting it into some sort of game that users might actively choose to play for entertainment. It is a rarer situation that this is possible but is sometimes achievable.

Another variation of this is altruism. One organisation created a computer game that asked users to determine how proteins fold based on their amino acid sequences. This is an important problem in medical research to help with drug discovery and biological science. The game was simplified and rules abstracted such that someone with no scientific training could complete the work. Large numbers of people were motivated to complete the challenge partially because it was gamified and fun but also from the charitable standpoint of doing something useful for society. Protein folding was a relatively difficult task at the time, although it has since been successfully completed by AI techniques.

Brute Force Computation

Unlike in the era of the Mechanical Turk, we now do genuinely have machines that are excellent chess players. The best computers are now essentially unbeatable by humans. Chess competitions are forced to go to great lengths to try and stop people using chess computers. Online chess matches often require webcams to be switched on and organisers compare moves made by human players to the output of common chess computers. If there are too many similarities they ban the relevant player for cheating.

Chess computers now exist that employ all forms of sophisticated AI methods, but the first highly successful machines that hit the headlines in the 1990s, particularly IBM's Deep Blue which became famous for beating then chess champion Gary Karparov, were not doing so much AI in the modern sense. Journalists of the time suggested Deep Blue was an advance in machine thought, but really the particularly notable feature was that the machine was just exceptionally fast for the time.

At the heart of Deep Blue was a mathematical function that could calculate how valuable any particular chess move was likely to be and assign a score to the move. Then it could calculate the value of a response that a chess player might make to its move. Then it would calculate the value of a move it might make as a response to the hypothetical player's response and so on. Deep Blue could iterate through an extraordinary number of potential chess moves and counter-moves, about 200 million per second, until it found the move with the best overall value as determined by its core chess evaluation function. It could also refer to a large database of known good moves.

Deep Blue would normally be classed as a form of AI, but it is really a massive brute force calculator. It rattles through every possible combination and permutation until it comes up with the best answer. It doesn't solve the problem by learning how to play chess as such.

Brute force computation can be the ultimate solution to some problems if you can afford to do it. There is a classic problem (with real world applications) called the travelling salesman problem, which is the calculation of the fastest way to travel between a number of towns.

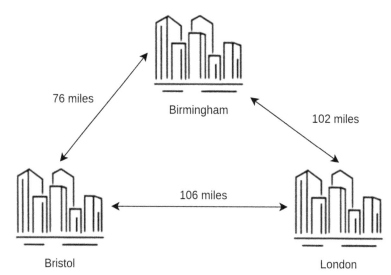

76 miles

Birmingham

102 miles

106 miles

Bristol

London

Figure 30: The travelling salesman problem, finding the shortest route to travel between many cities.

It's a much tougher problem than it looks when there are many towns as there are a large number of possible combinations of routes. If there are only 50 towns, then there are a staggering 3×10^{62} possible ways to route between them. This is an extremely large number that is of the scale of the number of atoms in a galaxy. This is well beyond the reasonable computational capability of any conventional computer system.

AI has long been applied to this problem, but will rarely come up with the best possible solution. At smaller scales, the problem is perfectly feasible by brute force computation though. With a dozen towns there are only 20 million ways to route between them, which is quite reasonable to attack with an inexpensive computer system. If you've just got the computational might available at reasonable cost to hammer through all the possible permutations, then that's the best way to solve the problem as the result will be flawless. However, with a large set of towns it becomes intractable and so currently we must usually resort to AI tricks that might produce an answer that is good enough, but not as good a solution as brute force.

SatNav software routinely solves a problem of the style of the travelling salesman and it is normally done on the cheapest built-to-a-price device that can be found with a woefully underpowered CPU. The software uses optimisations to reduce the number of permutations that must be inspected. These might be rules of thumb such as "stay on major roads" or "always try and travel in the direction of the destination city". If a few preferred routes are blocked the unit normally becomes dramatically slower as it suddenly has to try a vast number of combinations of side streets and minor roads.

The class of problems the travelling salesman falls into is known as nondeterministic polynomial-time complete or more succinctly as "NP-complete". A new advance in computing technology called quantum computing might challenge AI approaches by genuinely being able to provide the flawless solution to very large versions of this type of problem. These machines are now just emerging from research labs into the real world with commercial versions available for purchase. The essential difference between conventional computing and quantum machines is that a conventional computer has to try one possibility (or only a few) at once whereas a quantum machine can try all of them simultaneously. The challenge is that the machines are difficult to construct at scales that may beat a standard machine and are just on the edge of reaching the point where they may be useful.

Symbolic AI

Deep Blue may be put into the class of what is known as symbolic AI systems, that is almost entirely human designed logic that delivers the surface appearance of some underlying intelligence. This was typically the form of AI that was dominant until almost the year 2000. Symbolic AI is usually considered to be AI (the clue is in the name) but what is going on is not quite analogous to what recent machine learning systems are doing.

Symbolic AI may be very complex, but the structure and mechanism is in a form that is entirely human interpretable. An "expert system" is in the class of symbolic AI. This is essentially a decision tree (see Figure 31).

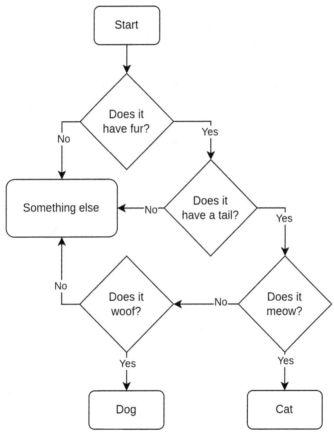

Figure 31 - A decision tree for differentiating dogs and cats

A machine may make decisions about what goes into the expert system but exactly how these systems achieve the end results is relatively easy to follow. The method of operation is human engineered. This is less the case with more recent AI systems where the system has devised more of its own method of operation without human intervention.

Similarly to a decision tree, very long lists of rules may also count as a form of symbolic AI. In early versions of voice assistant products it was common for the interactions to be programmed using templates. Someone would try to think through all of the variations in the way someone might phrase something and code them into the system:

{Please} add {AppointmentName} to {my or the} calendar

{Please} put {AppointmentName} on {my or the} calendar

{Will or Can} you put {AppointmentName} on {my or the} calendar {please}

{Please} make an appointment called {AppointmentName}

Programming long lists of rules is extremely tedious work but with enough employees and financing, a lot of the commonplace use cases can be covered by simply typing in most of the possibilities and then iteratively adding new variations as customers start interacting with the product outside of the programmed bounds. In some respects the customers assist with the process by gradually learning how to talk to the product and understanding what kinds of inputs it is likely to accept.

There are classes of programming languages that can assist symbolic AI. One of the most well-known languages of this type is Prolog, although the far more commonplace SQL language may also fall into the class. These are "declarative" languages. Most programming is currently performed in an "imperative" style where a specific sequence of instructions is to be followed in order. Declarative languages work quite differently. In languages like Prolog the programmer does not provide a sequence of instructions, a series of facts and the relationships between those facts are provided. A question can be asked of the system and it determines if it can logically answer the query using only the set of facts provided. For example, the fact Mittens is a cat may be provided and the fact that all cats are animals. The system can determine that Mittens is an animal without that specific piece of knowledge being programmed by following through the logical relationships between the facts. Prolog can deal with very complicated reasoning problems of this style.

Heuristics fall into the class of symbolic AI, that is rules of thumb that often lead to a reasonably optimised solution for complex problems. Heuristics have been used for some considerable time in automated circuit layout systems. The systems contain programmed rules that suggest placement of particular components in particular locations as a starting point based on the experience of engineers.

Circuit layout is a more complex variant of maze solving which has for some time benefited from heuristics. A well-known heuristic for solving certain kinds of mazes is to always keep one hand in contact with the wall (either left or right) and follow the wall around, never losing contact with the wall. The rule was developed by a human, a machine did not come up with it. The rule seems as if it results in some intelligence though as a machine using the programmed rule can solve a maze.

Symbolic AI isn't the "wrong" solution, after all it's unbelievably good at playing chess. Symbolic AI is the current best of breed solution for many problems and it wouldn't make sense to use anything else. One of the issues with symbolic AI though is the lack of flexibility with respect to anything that falls outside of the programmed rules. Symbolic AI systems struggle to generalise and adapt to situations that have not been seen previously. This is why other methods have recently gained more attention.

Exact Mathematical Solutions

Some problems have very robust and precise mathematical solutions. The solutions are the product of clever human thinking and nothing has been learnt by a machine at all. Where there is a known solution to a problem, it makes more sense to use that than a machine learning solution. It doesn't make sense to use AI to add two numbers together, it makes sense to use a calculator, but there can sometimes be pressure to describe an algorithmic solution as AI for marketing purposes when the methods are in vogue.

Algorithmic solutions can also be a better choice when there is a high cost to failure. When building a skyscraper with an investment totalling hundreds of millions it will be worth the expense to have an architect precisely calculate the true answer to the limits of the structure rather than have it reckoned by an AI.

AI systems can very often have unexpected behaviours and how they work can be unclear. Safety critical control systems might be best designed through formal methods, where every possibility is carefully thought out and every action the machine might take under every circumstance is specified. The algorithm used can be mathematically proven to be correct. There is never any ambiguity.

In many circumstances problems are just too complex to be solved by human mathematical reasoning (at least in any practical length of time). The costs of performing such reasoning may also be too high. If you're a supermarket trying to optimise the returns from selling cans of beans, it's not worth employing the world's finest team of top mathematicians to come back and tell you the AI solution was wrong, the true optimal answer makes you an extra penny of profit. Then there are the other 30,000 products in the store to consider. The near-enough optimisation solution from the AI is much cheaper to produce and more pragmatic. Context is key. If you're an aircraft manufacturer, you probably do want a team of mathematicians to spend three months formally proving the load on the wing is correct rather than having an AI say "trust me".

Monte Carlo Methods and Simulation

In this approach a simulator for a problem is built, inputs are tried at random and the effect on the output observed. Through repeated random sampling, patterns in the output come to light and the patterns converge on the perfect mathematical solution to the problem but are not completely accurate. The "near enough" solution though can be sufficient.

If you have a deck of cards and you want to know the probability of drawing an ace, you could solve the problem by simply drawing from the pack a large number of times and noting down how often an ace appears. You might be lucky and draw an ace twice in a row to start with and have an unduly high assessment of the chance of drawing that card. The more times the experiment is performed though, the frequency of appearance of an ace will start to converge on the correct statistical average. In this example the probability of drawing an ace is easy to calculate anyway and the experiment would be unnecessary, but many other problems are considerably tougher and do not have easy to calculate solutions. If a simulator for the problem can be easily built, a computer system can test it millions of times, drawing cards until the answer seems to be converging. Building the simulator can be considerably easier for some problems than figuring out the maths.

Einstein reputedly spent months determining the solution to a particular problem in physics related to Brownian motion regarding determining how far a particle will travel in a specific time. The mathematical methods by which the problem is solved are very complex and likely beyond the capability of most of us to understand. However, the same problem can be solved to a "near enough" standard with a simulator in under an hour from scratch by almost any programmer. The mathematics are of course more precise and the formal proof of correctness may be important, but if you don't need the absolutely correct answer then the simulator might be much easier.

Monte Carlo methods are widely employed in financial analysis to try and find optimal solutions to very complex statistical problems that are challenging to solve using precise mathematical methods. For example the technique is often used for the "value at risk" problem that tries to put a number on the extent of possible losses that might be incurred by a company. This can be very difficult to calculate for a problem such as investing where there may be many different business departments all conducting different types of investment strategies that might interact in complex ways and have all kinds of possible outcomes.

A spreadsheet of the probabilities of occurrence for all the risks the company is exposed to is compiled and then millions of different combinations of those risks arc tested at random. A profile can then be built of the probabilities of different levels of losses occurring based on different combinations of the risks. An assessment of the overall losses the company as a whole could incur can then be constructed.

Big Data

The term "Big Data" was in vogue before machine learning rose to prominence. Big data systems are all about very much what it says in the name, systems that have a lot of data. There is often a degree of overlap between what machine learning systems do and what big data systems do but the way results are obtained is not always the same.

Big data systems can seem as if they have a degree of intelligence, but without really having any intelligence as such. An example is web search engines and how they rank results. In the early days web search engines would use relatively simple techniques. The system would count how many times words appeared on pages, then present pages that contained a lot of references to whatever words were typed in by the user. This does indeed provide pages that match the user's search query but not in a particularly intelligent order. A website containing nothing but spam could rank higher than the most authoritative and high quality result on the internet because it simply repeats the relevant keywords more often than the authoritative page.

Google famously introduced "PageRank", which applied an extra dimension to the problem. It ranked pages not just by the words they contained but also by the popularity of the website as measured by how many other web sites pointed to it. The assumption being that good quality websites have a lot of other websites pointing to them and poor quality websites have few. This insight dramatically improved the quality of the results and was a great innovation. Now popular websites would move to the top of the rankings and it was much harder for spammers and marketeers to game the system by including lots of relevant words on their pages as there was the extra barrier of needing to create lots of other fake websites.

There was however another innovation that is less well known and possibly even more important to web search quality. The web search engines started recording all of the searches that were typed in and correlating that with which exact link the user ultimately clicked on. The theory being the links that got clicked by a lot of people were probably somewhat better links than those that were clicked fewer times. So next time someone types in that particular search, the web link that was clicked most often moves a little higher up the rankings. The best page should then gradually migrate to the top of the list.

This is roughly how a search engine knows what you want with such psychic precision (well relative to early search engines anyway that only used keywords). It's not necessarily any AI magic, but just the fact that a lot of users have typed in your search query before you and a lot of webmasters have set up links pointing to good pages. The web search engine is really a form of Mechanical Turk with some algorithmic spice added. The ghost in the machine is the wisdom of the crowds. The intelligence is the aggregate effect of lots of people all wanting the same information and each one has been a worker ant, doing a tiny part of the job of marking where the good information is located on the web.

The search engines are a giant database that stores all of these "votes" as to which is the good information and very rapidly tallies them when a query is entered. The top link that is returned is the democratic result of what all the people who typed in the same query thought about the results presented.

When using a streaming video platform, it is common for the platform to suggest what you might want to watch next. One method by which these suggestions can be produced is not necessarily by any particularly fancy machine learning algorithm, but just through the fact that the service has a lot of users. The service looks at the list of TV programmes that you enjoyed watching (perhaps you gave them a thumbs up) and then looks for someone else who also enjoyed watching what you did. It then simply suggests a new show that the other person liked that you have not yet watched. Somewhere out there in the world is your anonymous soul mate who likes to watch the same TV as you do. The system has just paired you up like a dating site and really the other person is suggesting to you what you should watch and not a computer. It's all a giant Mechanical Turk.

A similar idea is regularly used in online shopping. The system looks for other people who buy products that you rated highly and takes an item from their shopping list to suggest to you. It also forms correlations between products that people buy together frequently.

The results are tweaked this way and that. When a video streaming site finds your digital twin, how they select something from the other user's watch list may have some artificial intelligence applied to it over the top. Perhaps the system will select videos the other user has viewed most recently over those they viewed a long time ago. They might also aggregate and blend several users that are somewhat similar to you together. However, the core magic ingredient that makes the whole thing work is not any intelligence as such, it's that the service has a lot of users therefore it becomes statistically likely there is someone else out there who is just like you.

Big data systems can seem very intelligent, but in reality they just know all the answers to all of the questions. This is in the same way that a quiz expert may just have a tremendous memory and a great deal of patience for sitting down and memorising all the questions that are commonly asked in quizzes. This method works really well in some cases, but for a lot of problems it's just not practically possible to gather all of the answers or all of the answers may not exist. This is where AI can be needed to reason in the gaps.

A/B Testing

A/B testing is a very commonly used process of experimentation which produces a result like an optimisation system but there is not necessarily any AI involved at all.

An advertising company might come up with a number of factors it thinks might influence someone clicking on an advert. Clicking an advert generates revenue for the company and they seek to maximise that revenue. It is not known which factors are most relevant to the user clicking adverts. Perhaps the size of the adverts is most important or the positioning on the page. To test this the company deploys multiple versions of its software that are assigned to users at random. One group might receive a version with larger adverts and another group might receive a version with smaller but more numerous adverts. The two groups of users are then compared to determine which one clicked on the most adverts. Then another experiment is run where one group receives adverts on the left of the page and another on the right and the system determines which group clicked the most ads, or perhaps they were the same.

The features are iteratively changed in this way, one change at a time, until the number of ads clicked slowly rises.

This is an entirely human driven process involving no machine learning, but takes advantage of the large population of users available to continuously run optimisation experiments. A system with a relatively small number of users doesn't have this luxury as there are not enough user samples to produce statistically meaningful results in a reasonable period of time.

Building AI

When the training data has been acquired and the features selected, it is time to build the machine learning system. Neural networks are currently a major focus of popular media and research attention and consequently it is natural to assume this is the only option. Spectacular results have been achieved from neural networks with some very interesting and advanced applications. However, if the task being addressed is more mundane, another algorithm may be more appropriate for the problem and will often be much easier to use and deploy. The neural network isn't perfectly suited to every kind of task and other algorithms may perform better or have specific features that are desirable (such as explainability).

As a rule of thumb if the machine learning task is a business problem with training data of tabular form (e.g. a regression predicting sales volume of ice cream from the weather) it's likely some algorithm other than a neural network is suited to the task. Implementations of other algorithms will likely be tuned to the styles of inputs found in this kind of data, such as prices and categories and be able to directly produce the styles of output that may be expected. Use of a neural network may require a great deal more preparation of the data set, will be more complex to design and implement and not necessarily perform any better.

If all of the training data fits within a table of a few thousand rows and the answer to the problem is only needed by a small group of colleagues, it may be found that the tools already available within conventional spreadsheet software are entirely sufficient. Microsoft Excel and similar can run some types of machine learning for common business problems directly within the application (and also many other types of related statistical analysis). The ubiquitous spreadsheet may be all that is required and no specialist machine learning code is needed at all. To make use of the machine learning system the resulting spreadsheet file can simply be shared with those who require it.

As the volume of training data increases, a spreadsheet becomes unwieldy and eventually stops working. If the application needs to be shared by many people it may be impractical to pass a spreadsheet file around. If users of the system are outside the organisation, they may not have access to the relevant spreadsheet software to load in the file and may be excluded from using it. If a web or mobile phone app is being built to use the results of machine learning, then a spreadsheet is of little use as it is difficult to integrate into these platforms. For these kinds of applications, a software toolkit or library may be the answer.

Libraries of various descriptions are available for all popular programming languages that cover many common machine learning algorithms and use cases. The "Python" programming language is a very popular choice for machine learning (and data science generally) at the time of writing and there are several machine learning libraries to choose from. One of the most commonly used libraries is "scikit-learn" which includes dozens of algorithms and variants. A large number of tutorials and examples can be found on the web for this library. If the reader is interested in learning how to build AI systems in practice, learning a little Python would be a good starting place.

To perform machine learning using a software library, usually the training data is pre-prepared into a collection of files in a common format that is easily read in software, such as CSV (Comma-Separated Values) or JSON. A short program is written that first reads all of the data into memory. Next the training data is split into the features (e.g. the weather on any specific day) and the expected answers (how many ice creams were sold). These two sets are sometimes referred to as the X and Y sets respectively. There is a corresponding entry in the Y set for each entry in the X set. An appropriate algorithm is selected from the software library and the data applied to it. Training is then run, which is often referred to as "fitting" to the model.

Often software libraries will have some helpful built in features to assist with avoiding overfitting and can automatically split the data into a training set and an unseen test/validation set before running the training by sampling the data at random. It is possible to select how much data is placed into each specific bucket before the training is run. After the training phase the software library is able to produce statistics indicating the performance of the model and how well it has worked i.e. whether it has been able to find relevant patterns in the data. If the model does work as well as hoped, then changes to the training data or feature selection may be needed or a different algorithm may be tested.

The model is now held in memory, but will be discarded when the program terminates. The developer can save the successfully trained model to a file. This is usually in some proprietary format that is specific to the software library chosen. It is not guaranteed that any other library would be able to read it and the model file will often only work with the library that originally created it. Some standards for exchanging models in open formats are emerging though.

The developer can now write a separate program that can read the model back in from disk and perform inference. Once back in memory, predictions can be run against the model. Features are applied and it produces its guess as to the output. The trained model file can now be integrated into the end application, for example it can be integrated into a web app or mobile phone app to provide predictions to end-users based on input data. The model file can also be shared on the web such that other developers interested in the same problem do not need to perform the training phase.

When it comes to dealing with media such as images, audio and natural language text, it is more likely a neural network based machine learning approach will be selected as most of the research effort is focussing on applications built with these techniques. The way neural networks are developed can be a little more complex than many other approaches depending on the exact application. It is entirely feasible to write a neural network from scratch and this can be achieved in only a few dozen lines of code, however more typically the developer will choose to use a "framework". This is essentially a software library but includes a more heavyweight structure for building an application and a suite of tools in addition to an implementation of the core machine learning algorithm. The two most commonly used neural network frameworks for Python at the time of writing are TensorFlow and PyTorch (with the latter starting to gain somewhat more traction presently) but others exist. As with scikit-learn, there is no shortage of tutorial and educational materials available for these frameworks on the web for free.

Machine learning with images and video often requires significant amounts of computation due to the high dimensionality of the input and some form of hardware acceleration may be beneficial. The developer may have to wait hours (or days) for training to complete which slows down iterations of the software development cycle. Hardware acceleration, such as GPUs, can significantly assist with this problem. Acceleration devices can be very complex to work with and require specialist coding techniques best implemented by experts familiar with the relevant hardware to get the highest levels of performance out of it. Without an in-depth understanding of precisely how the hardware works, it is easy to waste potential and achieve only disappointing performance. Machine learning frameworks will usually include an interface to common kinds of AI acceleration hardware as standard with all of the hard work already done. Integration with accelerators is one of the key benefits of using a framework.

A framework allows a neural network to be built from a description of the network structure. For example the developer will specify how many layers it should have, exactly how the layers should be connected together and which activation function should be used. The framework will then construct the network to the provided specification and automatically wire it up so values flow from one neuron to the next. Specialist layers can also be added such as convolution layers that are considered helpful for working with images. Some networks can have quite complex structures and the framework may already have the current best known solutions to certain problems configured as standard which can be a significant time saver.

The developer may next have to configure a "loss function" which informs the training how to measure the difference between the output the network actually produced and the output it should have produced as defined by the training examples. A number of standard loss function types (which have differing trade-offs and benefits) are usually provided.

The frameworks typically include facilities for converting common types of training inputs into the range of values acceptable to the network input. Neural networks only deal in floating point numbers, often in the range of -1 to +1. The application though may call for text or images to be input. The frameworks include convenience features for enumerating dictionaries of words into numbers and dealing with embeddings. They might also include features for converting the colour model of images into a continuous single dimensional value in the appropriate range. These conversions are relatively awkward to code manually and it is helpful to have this handled by the framework.

Features are included for managing training data, such as splitting into training and test sets, but also assisting with managing appropriate training data batch sizes so the data can fit within the memory of the GPU or other accelerator. The framework will usually include features to help with data normalisation. A training data set may include images of varying sizes but the neural network will only accept uniformly sized images. The framework can assist with automatically resizing images to a consistent size that the network can accept. Frameworks can also include automated data augmentation features to improve the robustness of the learning.

Frameworks regularly include some form of built in visualisation features that can help with displaying selections of images from the training data in a grid. If the neural network is producing an image, it may be able to display the output images to show the progress of machine learning as it is occurring. This allows for monitoring of a long running training process and learning can be stopped early if it does not seem to be working as expected.

Using a framework limits the scope of how the application may be deployed as the application can only run on the hardware that the framework supports. There may be some situations where this is not ideal. Running a smaller neural network on a very limited embedded device (such as a battery powered sensor) might be one such example as the framework may be far too resource intensive to be installed on the target platform. In which case coding a neural network by hand might be the right answer. It is possible to develop a neural network and train it using a framework and then transfer the resulting model to a hand coded neural network on a less capable device for inference. Some frameworks are available for the more popular, moderately powerful embedded platforms, however the support is not universal.

It is possible mobile phones may not be able to execute heavyweight frameworks intended for desktop PCs and servers but usually the mobile market (meaning Android and iOS) is relatively well served in this regard as there is high demand for AI applications in this space. Consequently the largest vendors usually produce "light" versions of frameworks or a specialist mobile version that can run successfully on these platforms. The catch is the mobile version may lack some features present on the desktop version and care needs to be taken that development is done within the scope of the services that the mobile framework can offer. Additionally it needs to be recognised that the average mobile phone typically has much less RAM and a slower CPU than a desktop PC. Storage space is also more likely to be at a premium and cannot be upgraded on some phones. The user will appreciate the model being kept to a reasonable size which implies it may need to be less capable than a corresponding version for a desktop PC.

Most mobile phones now have some form of GPU that can in theory be used for AI acceleration. Specialist AI specific hardware is also arriving for mobile devices. The market though supports a more diverse range of architectures than desktop PCs with lots of disparate hardware and some of the chip vendors are not open about providing relevant documentation. A framework may be able to help with identifying and providing acceleration on a diverse range of mobile device hardware where possible.

Where a mobile device (or embedded system) is simply insufficient to run a model, the option always remains of running it remotely in a data centre over the internet. However it may be preferable to run a model directly on the user's own device where possible to avoid the developer incurring processing costs every time the application is used.

At the time of writing, methods of developing AI change quickly and the market is moving at a fast pace. It is likely newer and easier to use methods will become available shortly, particularly techniques for simplifying the design, training and deployment of neural networks.

AI Risks

There's a concept called "Artificial General Intelligence" or AGI, which is the idea that an intelligent agent system might be produced that can accomplish any task that a human is able to perform. This then leads to the question of what if the AGI becomes more intelligent than us humans? Perhaps it achieves some kind of self awareness and maybe doesn't like having us around. The end result of the chain of thought is existential risk: roving bands of terminators and the war against the machines.

AGI delivers a dramatic plot for fiction but back in the real world we are a long way from super-intelligent AIs being any form of realistic concern. Large language models might seem like an AGI but they really have only a thin veneer of intelligence. LLMs have a lot of human written information at their disposal and are great editors and summarisers, but probe below the surface and the systems don't have much more than a basic ability to reason yet. The intelligence of these machines is getting gradually deeper as the models become larger and the training sets more expansive, but as much as they are useful they remain spectacularly dumb at the moment. There are more immediate concerns though surrounding AI that might impact us on a more near-term basis.

Adversarial Attacks

Adversarial attacks are methods deliberately designed to confound AI systems and cause them to operate in ways other than intended. One example that has been successfully produced several times by security researchers is construction of a special shape that can be printed out and held up which causes a human detecting camera to fail to notice that an obvious and undisguised person is present in the scene. This might be used maliciously by a criminal to bypass a security camera for example. The printed shape is a form of digital camouflage that is ineffective against people but completely confuses an AI system.

The way researchers have constructed these specific shapes is by themselves using machine learning systems working against classifiers. The adversarial systems iteratively make modifications to an image of a person until the confidence level of the classifier that it can see a human begins to decline and ultimately falls below a trigger threshold. It then incorrectly reports there is no person present in the field of view of the camera.

In San Francisco, a number of groups that object to the self-driving taxi services have discovered that placing a traffic cone on the bonnet of the cars causes them to come to halt and refuse to move. Several groups of vandals have been going round immobilising the vehicles. The exact reason the vehicles stop under this condition hasn't been disclosed by the manufacturers but it may of course be that they are simply programmed to detect a foreign object anywhere on the vehicle body and immediately halt, which might be a wise safety precaution. If the car drove with an unsecured object anywhere on the exterior it might become dislodged and injure a passing pedestrian when the car is driving at speed. It might fall into the road and do damage to a vehicle driving behind that runs over it. The object might affect the vehicle safety systems by obscuring the view of sensors. Equally though it may be that the vehicle has no capability to detect foreign objects on the bodywork and the car sees something else entirely. It might think it sees a traffic cone in the street that it cannot work out how to manoeuvre around because it always stays in a fixed position in front of the camera and the vehicle comes to a halt for that reason.

The traffic cone is a comically crude form of adversarial attack but is an example that has actually been deployed in practice by malicious actors against real AI systems in the wild with the intent of causing disruption. It demonstrates that the concept is not just a theoretical concern and that motivated people are prepared to seek ways to cause these systems to misbehave. Causing self-driving cars to come to a halt in awkward places is nuisance behaviour, however it may be imagined that more dangerous forms of attack might exist. Perhaps it may be possible for some criminal intent on malice to craft a special shape, as in the case of the people detector, that causes a self-driving car to fail to notice a red traffic signal even though the signal is obviously visible to a person. An attacker may be able to gain unsupervised access to a safety critical product by leasing it for a period of time and then tapping into the software to investigate methods to thwart its safety systems.

Other kinds of adversarial attacks might just cause widespread disruption, for example if someone discovers some advantage that can be gained to game a system by confounding an AI. It might be that a city deploys emergency vehicle detecting cameras that turn traffic lights green and someone figures out how to make their private car appear to be an ambulance to an AI system. Such a hack might then spread like wildfire on the internet and cause streets to be jammed when thousands of inconsiderate people print out the relevant shape and stick it to their dashboard.

For the majority of AI applications, the possibility of adversarial attacks isn't really a major issue, an attack will just cause some minor inconvenience to a user and they will reset the faulty equipment. Perhaps a software update will be issued if the attack is particularly prevalent. However for applications with a safety or security consideration, such as vehicles and CCTV, adversarial attacks could be a potential concern. Care needs to be taken to ensure such safety critical applications are hardened against these kinds of attacks.

One way of doing this is for the developer to be aware of the malicious techniques and attempt to produce adversarial examples themselves in advance of an attacker doing it i.e. get ahead of the game. Once a successful traffic light detector is produced, the developer should try and craft an adversarial training system that can confound it, then teach the traffic light detector to be able to avoid whatever tricks the adversarial AI came up with. This is exactly the same kind of technology used in GANs that are currently popular for generative AI and tools are easily available.

There are more technically involved methods of guarding against adversarial attacks such as "feature squeezing" which attempts to reduce the sensitivity of a model to noise. This causes spurious information added to the input to be less likely to make it ignore any correct information it is seeing and suddenly flip the decision made by a classifier. Another technique known as "null labelling" can make it harder to transfer adversarial examples produced on one data set to another where the attacker does not have access to the data set originally used to train the classifier.

Another method is to use a backup detector that has been produced in a different manner. Multiple different traffic light detectors operating independently based on different training data would make it more challenging to produce a single adversarial example that fools all of them simultaneously. The detectors would work as an ensemble and take a vote on whether a traffic light could be seen. Other classifiers might work in an entirely different way, for example detecting the general layout of a road intersection where traffic lights are commonly present and watching the behaviour of other vehicles but not actually looking for a traffic light as such. If the system observes a location with a layout that implies a traffic light should be present, even though it can't see one, then it should slow down and drive more defensively.

Many self-driving car implementations are also backed-up by a map of where traffic lights should be located (although not all implementations) and if it cannot locate the signal in the expected place then it comes to a halt or drives more conservatively. A successful adversarial attack would then need to simultaneously work against multiple different sensors with completely different modes of operation, which would be harder to achieve.

Bias in Training Sets

A major component dictating the quality of a machine learning system is the quality of the training data. How well the system performs depends on the number of examples it has seen for each possible situation. A common problem is that the number of examples easily available to a developer for each situation is not necessarily even.

One of the most frequently cited bias examples is in face identification systems. The developers of the systems often collect training data from only their own country, as that is most easily available. This data naturally has fewer examples of faces that are not in the majority ethnic group. The system then consequently performs less well on minority group faces. This can have real world social consequences such as ethnic minority groups being misidentified more frequently by security systems with particular groups then disproportionately bearing the costs of that misidentification.

The problem is not just with socially embarrassing encounters with law enforcement but also with more mundane day-to-day inconveniences. For example, if a workplace door entry system that relies on face recognition cannot reliably recognise your face, that means calling over a security guard to manually open the door. It might take an unacceptably long time to persuade an understaffed security desk to attend a fully automated location, causing you to be late for work. An airport fast-entry system that doesn't work with your face means joining an hour-long queue every time with the frustration of watching everyone else sail past with ease.

The solution to training bias is clearly to ensure the data set is as evenly representative as is possible to avoid causing inconvenience to users. However, that may mean higher costs to acquire appropriately evenly balanced data sets where data has to be specially sought out as opposed to taking advantage of what can be found for free. Some equipment manufacturers may decide they do not want to pay this cost. Organisations installing the equipment might decide to buy less robust versions because they are cheaper. Regulation and certification may be needed to ensure that equipment in public facing roles provides even and fair service to all.

Training data biases in AI systems may often be accidental but biases may also be introduced intentionally into systems. This may be as a result of corporate policies. For example a generative system may be specifically coded to avoid saying anything negative about major brands for fear of litigation or loss of advertising revenue. Such speech may be entirely legal, accurate and warranted but an AI company may see it as not worth their trouble and avoid the area entirely. A system may also of course be coded to avoid saying anything negative about the brand that created it or possibly even to surreptitiously promote that brand. This may make it difficult to obtain a fair and unbiased review of a product if the system will not divulge any negative aspects.

Company policies may be entirely proportionate from the perspective of the company producing the system. However a user has a reasonable expectation that a system is behaving in an unbiased manner. Systems need to be able to state what corporate policies they are complying with and inform the user when the system has been prevented from producing unbiased output through compliance with a policy.

Job Displacement

It is quite likely many jobs will be replaced by AI systems. The logistics industry is moving towards a position where it may soon be possible for a product to travel from the factory gates to your front door with no human involvement at all. Self-driving trucks are now feasible. Robot cargo loaders are in use that can place a container on a ship without a human operator. It is possible to sail a ship with full automation. Warehouses are increasingly using robots to move items around. Small robots exist that can move orders from a warehouse to a customer's front door. It may be that soon few people will be needed in this industry at all.

Many fast food chains no longer take orders at a counter with a human cashier but either require or strongly encourage customers to order through a provided touchscreen device or app on their personal phone. This is not an example of AI but is an example of where automation has quite suddenly appeared on the scene and replaced human jobs on a very large scale over a short period of time. It was until recently commonplace to see a bank of a dozen cashiers in a fast food location but now there may be only one or two who are mainly involved with assembling the orders and handing them to customers rather than dealing with the order taking and payment. In the kitchen there are some quite amazing AI driven robots now available that can cook food. One of the most sophisticated is aimed at the fast food industry and can prepare french fries and cook a burger just the same as a human. These robots are rarely used currently but this part of the job may be on the cusp of change with robots at least partially doing the food preparation. Robots will also do the job more consistently and quickly than a human and without needing a break.

The retail industry is one of the largest employers in the world and is also one of the industries that has seen the most automation. The checkout assistant is largely on the way out and will become a job of the past. A key remaining job in retail is stocking shelves, however it seems this could be successfully automated with improved design.

Farming has seen dramatic advances in automation over the centuries. This has often come as a matter of necessity as once plentiful farm labourers have opted for other occupations. In a few cases the picking of crops has been automated for some considerable time (such as harvesting wheat) but more often this task has fiercely resisted the robots. Picking delicate fruit such as strawberries and grapes has until recently been impractical by mechanical means. This has resulted in the employment of armies of seasonal labour performing strenuous work. However, new robots are now coming onto the market that can successfully handle the task. Sophisticated machines equipped with AI driven camera systems can now identify ripe fruit and figure out how to grasp it without damage.

Weed control robots are now available. These robots can cover a large acreage and automatically detect the difference between crops and weeds using sophisticated camera systems. The weeds can actually be targeted and destroyed individually using lasers. This has the side benefit of obviating the need for herbicides that can cause environmental problems and be unpopular with consumers with a preference for organic food.

Customer services may be due some considerable automation. Intuitively, LLMs in the form of chatbots seem like an obvious automation choice for answering customer queries. A variety of chatbots are indeed currently deployed, but customers will usually do almost anything to avoid talking to them as they are universally near useless. The grade of chatbot that is most usually operational is particularly simplistic, often just watching for keywords. All chatbots currently do is present an unwanted and challenging barrier to the customer figuring out how to get hold of an actual human.

Leading edge chatbots are getting better though and are becoming good at understanding the meaning of what the customer requested. However, delivering an intelligent chatbot with a genuine capability to behave as a customer services agent is a difficult task. Where chatbots might do well in the short term is acting more as an advanced search engine, directing customers to pre-written information in product literature. Asking product questions is one key reason why people call customer services.

Prophecies about future job losses from automation have to date usually ended up being overstated. The jobs market tends to shift with new types of jobs being created as old ones disappear. Hundreds of thousands of people used to be employed as telephone switchboard operators, but that was automated away decades ago. New jobs appeared to replace the old jobs. Automation can also create new jobs by making the function cheaper and therefore enabling more of it to be done. There used to be a job of filing clerk that employed a lot of people but filing of information is now rarely done manually. Instead there is the new job of database engineer and there are a lot of those as the demand for information storage and organisation has increased dramatically as the cost of the process has gone down.

Inaccurate Results

Large language models have been infamous for generating factual inaccuracies as a matter of routine. The problem is the models quite often produce correct information but intermittently do not. When models produce correct information many times in a row, the systems build up credibility with users who then inadvisably come to the conclusion that the model must be infallible. LLMs though regularly produce answers that seem plausible but are entirely fictional. Such factual inaccuracies have come to be known as "hallucinations".

One of the issues is LLMs don't use hedging language in the way people do. LLMs are just confidently wrong. If you stopped someone on the street for directions and they said "straight over the roundabout and it's the 2nd left", you assume the instructions are correct as the response is confidently worded. However, if they say "oh, I think it might be the 2nd left as I remember" you would treat the instructions with more scepticism as the language sounds uncertain. People have a sense of how good their recollection is and convey that through patterns of speech. LLMs just confidently blurt out entirely inaccurate information as if it were absolute fact.

LLMs are particularly good at producing deceiving text. This is not intentional design as such but more of a side-effect of the way the systems work. The models have a great deal of expertise at their disposal and can produce responses that sound very convincing even when not accurate. The models can get into the correct ballpark of the right answer and say it with conviction. A lawyer was caught citing legal precedents in a court case that were entirely fictional and manufactured by an LLM. The models just sound so plausible even to those who should know better.

The confident inaccuracy of LLMs can be particularly problematic as the models contain information about real people. If an LLM is asked about scandals a politician may have been involved in, if there are none it will gladly invent one that sounds very convincingly like exactly the sort of thing an unscrupulous politician would do. The issue is then that people may take action based on that inaccuracy which could have real world consequences.

There is a long running satirical newspaper called "The Onion" that produces fictional news reports based around celebrity figures and real world events. The articles are written with the tone of a serious news publication. Even though the content is outlandish and comedic, people unfamiliar with the nature of the publication regularly link to the articles as if they were genuine authoritative news output. Similarly people unfamiliar with the propensity of LLMs to generate fictional content will likely quote it as fact.

There is currently no reliable method of automated fact checking that can confirm that what an LLM says is actually true. The systems very much rely on the assumption that the users will check the results themselves against credible sources. There are technologies that aim to provide links to sources where the LLM scraped the information from that may go some way towards mitigating this, but it still requires a user to diligently follow up on the research and not just lazily copy whatever the LLM said. That might prove to be too great an expectation of the average person.

Intermittent AI inaccuracies are not just an issue for LLMs. Some forms of self-driving car are not completely reliable and require driver monitoring. The problem with these systems is that they most often work reliably, but not absolutely always. If the system constantly made mistakes, the driver would be vigilant and alert at all times, but when the systems normally drive to a high standard but occasionally do not, then the drivers become complacent. The driver is faced with the boring task of monitoring a situation where nothing is happening for hour after hour and their attention inevitably wavers. It has not been unknown for drivers to be found asleep whilst being driven by a car that they are supposed to be monitoring.

Spam Generation

The age of unlimited generative AI has brought with it the age of unlimited spam generation. Web pages can now be written with ease. There have for a long time been farms of poor quality web pages typed up by low wage contractors with the intent of drawing in users. Web search engines have been fighting against this problem for decades. The pages do not provide the user with the information they are looking for but are strewn with adverts and the site owners hope an unsuspecting user may click on the adverts whilst they are wasting their time with the useless content.

The cost of producing a web page that appears superficially as if it might contain useful information has now dropped dramatically with generative AI. A web page can be produced for a fraction of a penny. It is only once the user invests time reading the page in detail that they realise the content is nonsense or poor quality. The amount of accidental advertising revenue a spammer may generate from their investment is now likely much higher than the cost of producing the page. When the economics swing such that revenue is much greater than cost, more spam content may be produced.

There has been some concern that the future web may become completely filled with generative AI content and consequently become completely useless. I would suspect though that search engines will probably ultimately win the war and manage to solve this problem as there is a considerable financial incentive to do so. If the web becomes of no use to people then there is no market for search engines which are one of the most lucrative businesses on the planet. If the search engines can sufficiently down-rank machine generated content then it effectively becomes invisible to real people and the web remains useful. It doesn't matter if most of the content on the web is machine generated if humans never have to see it and it's just bots talking to themselves.

Another suggested risk is that generative AI may itself become useless because the training data usually originates from the web. At the time of writing most web pages are human written, however it may be the case that in the future the majority of web pages become machine written. This may cause a situation where generative AI is reading mainly its own content and gradually becomes poisoned by being trained on nonsense it has itself produced. Presumably though generative AI companies will produce methods of solving this.

A further problem is the generation of fictitious social media accounts to amplify a message. This is sometimes known as "astroturfing", meaning a fake grass-roots campaign manufactured by a marketing company to give the appearance of spontaneously emerging public support of a form that benefits the sponsor. Generative AI can create a convincing photo of a person, easily write an appropriate biography and produce some authentic looking comments and posts. Hence any number of online accounts that appear superficially to be real people can be generated to "like", upvote and agree with whatever message the bot owner prefers, therefore giving the impression of a lot of support for a statement where there is actually little interest at all.

Fake social media accounts are not a new problem. They have been produced in large numbers previously by scraper bots that steal a photo from here, a name from there and some comments and posts from elsewhere and then weave them together. These accounts have been relatively easy to prove as fictitious by locating the original content and demonstrating the bot version is a copy. Generative AI can produce new fresh content though that cannot be found elsewhere on the web making that specific detection technique less successful.

The use of generative AI will probably always be possible to detect for a motivated investigator. There will be limits to how convincing a generative system can make a sock-puppet account seem to be. It will sometimes make mistakes that will go undetected by the author as they will likely not wish to spend a great deal of time reviewing all of their own content. With sufficient investigation a fake persona will fall apart. It would only take a few bots to be detected in a group to cast doubt on the validity of the scale of support for the promoted message. However, generative AI may give the superficial impression of widespread support for a message to the casual observer and most people do not take the time to investigate the veracity of a claim in any great detail. This may exacerbate the problem of fake social media bots.

Explainable AI

Most machine learning systems operate as a black box. A number of inputs go into the box and a decision based on those inputs comes out. What happens inside the box? Who knows. This lack of understanding of the process an AI system is using can cause a problem in a number of instances.

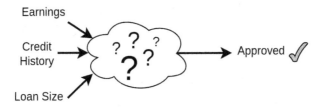

Figure 32 - A black box AI system. The method by which it arrives at a decision is unknown.

A familiar example is the situation with credit scoring. Credit evaluation systems are often built using machine learning techniques. When reviewing a credit application a bank will take a number of factors into account. Those factors may be the income of the applicant, the size of the loan amount, the number of times they have missed a payment previously or the amount of outstanding credit the applicant already has elsewhere.

All of these factors are fed into a machine learning black box (such as a regression system) and a number comes out. A high number means the applicant is credit worthy and a low number means the application will be declined. However, if the applicant is declined all the bank often has to say about the reasoning is that it was "to do with credit scoring". The reasoning of the machine learning black box has not been reverse engineered.

The credit applicant however may not be satisfied by this. They may demand an explanation. Should they wait until they have more income? Should they ask the bank for less money? No one has any idea. It's frustrating to the customer that the bank refuses to provide an explanation and they will almost certainly decide to look elsewhere for credit but as well as the bank potentially unnecessarily losing a customer, there may also be legal consequences. The bank may be required to prove that its lending process is reasonable, fair and not discriminatory. If the bank has absolutely no idea what their lending process actually is, then they may find themselves outside of legal compliance.

Safety critical applications may not be able to (or should not) use AI if they cannot clearly explain, with evidence, why it makes the decisions that it does. If an aircraft manufacturer cannot explain why their new autopilot unexpectedly decided to drop altitude by 1000 feet then they may find themselves facing unnerved customers and an unimpressed aviation regulator.

Even relatively mundane applications can benefit from explanations. Why did your AI driven smart thermostat decide to turn on the heating during an apparently warm day and waste money? Perhaps you are due an explanation such that you can find the fault.

Some AI techniques can deliver explanations naturally. A decision tree can be easily reverse engineered into an explanation (see Figure 33).

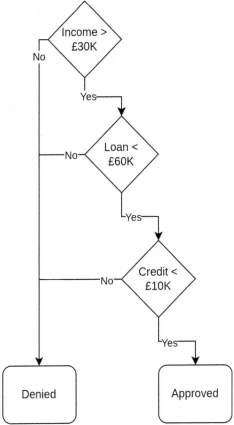

Figure 33 - It is easy to reverse engineer a
decision tree to explain the decision it makes.

To provide an explanation, a system simply needs to walk through the decision tree again and note which branches were taken. The explanation is: if income is greater than £30,000, loan amount is less than £60,000 and other outstanding credit is less than £10,000 then the application is approved. Where credit was declined, the application went the wrong way on one of the branches.

For the great majority of systems though, it is not so simple and the more complex they are, the less explainable they are. Why did a neural network composed of 100 million neurons decide to do what it did? How did it know the picture it was looking at was a cat? What infinitesimally small and subtle contribution did each of those neurons make to the final decision? Who knows. However, hope is not lost.

One method for neural networks is called Layer-Wise Relevance Propagation (LRP). In this technique a neural network is asked to produce its prediction. The path through the network is traced backwards and the specific neurons that had the largest contribution to the result are calculated using an analysis technique. The pixels that are attached to those pathways that had a large contribution to the output are then noted and an image can be produced showing exactly what the neural network was particularly concentrating on. For example it might highlight pixels on the ears and tail as being what it used to determine it is a picture of a cat.

In the case of the aircraft that dropped 1000 feet, it might highlight that it thought it saw an object in the video feed that might be another aircraft and it dropped altitude to avoid it. For the credit application it might highlight the input referring to the applicant's income. The income level that is acceptable may not be precisely described by the analysis, but it demonstrates that this is where the majority of the problem is.

Another technique is the system can highlight training examples that it thinks are somewhat like the particular test instance it has been presented with. For example it may highlight examples of bad credit applications that it was given in training that are similar to the specific application it has been asked to look at. This is somewhat like a lawyer citing previous similar case law to a judge as reasons why a defendant should receive a particular judgement. If the judge agrees that the cases are indeed similar, then there may be a similar outcome.

Counterfactual searches can also be used where a system plays around with the inputs to determine which one might have an impact. For example it might increase or decrease the credit applicant's income in small steps and see if that has much of an effect. You may in fact be a counterfactual AI explainer without realising it. Your car insurance premium is likely calculated by an AI system. You have probably played about with the mileage, coverage and the excess amount to see what effect it has on the price outcome.

A novel approach with large language models is that they can be simply asked why they produced the answer they did as they have an intrinsic language capability and can provide an explanation in English words just like a person. The answers are not always correct or useful (just like a person), but are at least trivial to produce. That is however a method that is unique to that specific kind of AI product.

Non-explainable AI is useful in many contexts. An entertainment AI program doesn't need to provide any explanation as to how it did what it did. An AI image manipulation system doesn't need to provide an explanation, if it works then great, if it doesn't then perhaps try again. Many applications are fairly benign and if they fail to produce the expected result then it doesn't matter. However, for systems that have serious consequences for people, explanations are required. This may also become something that is enshrined in law in some countries. There is academic philosophical discussion about the "right to an explanation" and the European GDPR may arguably include such a right in a narrowly defined context.

AI Hardware

AI training and inference can be performed on any conventional computing device. No specialist hardware is needed at all. All popular frameworks for AI support use of conventional CPUs with no issue. There is no AI operation that specifically requires or cannot be performed without the use of specialist hardware. Everything works on regular CPUs.

Not every AI problem requires a monster sized computer. A business problem that fits on a spreadsheet isn't going to need any significant resources. Machine learning on a few hundred rows of data will train to completion in a few seconds using a laptop found in a supermarket bargain bin. The computational might required depends on the number of dimensions at the input, the complexity of the system (such as the size of the neural network) and how much training data is used. The AI products hitting the headlines often involve millions of input dimensions, billions of neurons and terabytes of training data. This requires serious computational power to handle and often that means dozens or hundreds of very expensive high power servers running for days, weeks or months.

Using a conventional CPU for AI is almost always the preferable approach where possible because the hardware is easily available and does not suffer from the restrictions that specialist hardware imposes. Conventional CPUs are easier to program than specialist hardware and are considerably more flexible. The same hardware can be put to alternative uses when not required for AI purposes but specialist hardware is more rigid, either being entirely single purpose or otherwise poorly suited alternative applications.

Specialist AI hardware is only worth considering where it can offer a price/performance advantage. The advantage specialist hardware offers over conventional CPUs will always vary and change. Currently specialist hardware (particularly GPUs) have the economic edge for AI training and inference at large scales. Large arrays of conventional CPUs though are an entirely viable option from a technical perspective that may become more cost competitive in the future.

The cost of any particular solution often depends on the effects of commoditisation in the IT equipment marketplace. Even though CPUs may be less efficient, they can be more price competitive if produced for the mass market where the alternatives are not. Commoditisation trends in the consumer electronics space have already and will likely continue to be a major driving factor in how AI is achieved. Another major commoditisation influence is the cloud computing data centre market that provides largely hidden but vast-scale internet services to consumers and businesses. Whatever technologies are needed for the average business server application will also drive economies of scale. The scale of production influences the price of the devices and as a consequence the price/performance characteristics of the technologies. Technically inefficient solutions can end up becoming more cost efficient than technically superior solutions because of commoditisation effects, which depends on what the influencing markets want to buy.

Power consumption is another factor that can influence whether specialist AI hardware makes sense. The lifetime electricity cost of running a server can often cost as much as the server hardware itself. If two devices cost the same to buy and have the same performance but one has lower power consumption over the other then that can tip the balance for a large business that buys many hundreds or thousands of chips. Power consumption is also a very important factor in mobile, where devices run from batteries.

Some conventional CPUs are now emerging that include elements of specialist AI hardware as a standard feature and the performance gap between a mainstream commodity CPU as found in any regular off-the-shelf PC and specialist AI hardware might eventually narrow rendering the latter moot.

GPUs

GPUs (Graphics Processing Units) are currently the most popular device for AI training and inference. This is due to the commoditisation effects driven by the computer games industry, which has brought down the prices of this specific device. Many millions of GPUs are sold every year and one can be found in the PC of most serious computer game enthusiasts. GPUs were never originally designed to be and still are not the most efficient device for AI training applications, but represent a reasonable price versus performance balance, especially for the individual and small organisation. A GPU will often deliver about a 5 - 10x cost advantage over buying the equivalent compute in the form of conventional x86 CPUs. More recent GPUs have included features specifically to try and accelerate AI performance but 3D graphics remains the core market.

The suitability of GPUs for AI is purely a coincidence in that the operations required for neural network training and inference turned out to be reducible to the same mathematical operations used in 3D graphics. Largely this means matrix arithmetic, which GPUs excel at and is used heavily in both domains. Originally researchers figured out how to convert AI operations into 3D graphics but later the GPU manufacturers, sensing new markets, added features to support the required AI operations directly without necessitating a conversion to graphics first. Most popular AI programming frameworks support the use of GPU acceleration.

GPUs perform a kind of computing called "vector processing". A conventional CPU operates on one (or a small range of values) at once but GPUs can perform the same calculation on thousands of numbers at the same time. The catch is it has to be exactly the same calculation and not a different calculation performed on each number. This mode of operation works very well for matrix arithmetic but poorly for other types of workload where a conventional CPU is superior. Many CPUs now also include some kind of vector processing operations but they do not usually work on such large volumes of numbers at once as a GPU can handle.

GPUs also apply a number of other tricks to improve performance. They normally use much faster (and more expensive) memory than that which is typically supplied with a CPU. They are also very good at hiding memory latency. Main memory is comparatively slow compared with the rate at which a GPU can operate. GPUs are designed to process many operations in parallel. The devices can process an operation, then when that operation requires use of slow memory, it is put aside and the GPU processes a different operation whilst the memory gets around to responding to the original operation. It then returns to the original operation later when the memory comes back with the needed information. This trick works well provided that multiple operations do not have cascading interdependencies, that is if the next operation is not dependent on the result of the previous operation that is still pending waiting on the memory. AI operations can often successfully work within that limitation and are hence are a good match for GPUs.

Most GPUs can actually execute conventional software and be used as a general-purpose CPU. However, the performance in this mode is usually poor when compared with a conventional CPU of equal cost. Some software uses a GPU as an accelerator by effectively using it as a secondary conventional processor. This wouldn't make a lot of economic sense (another conventional CPU would be cheaper) except that many PCs are equipped with a GPU as standard for use with 3D games and it may as well be used if it is available otherwise it is just sitting idle and going to waste. It only makes sense as the GPU is a sunk cost. The particular economic advantage of a GPU arises when it can be used in the vector processing mode as is the case with matrix arithmetic for AI operations.

Systolic Arrays

The vector architecture of commodity GPUs is good but not optimal for AI operations and various attempts have been made to produce specialist devices that correct the deficiencies. GPUs also include features specific to 3D graphics that can never be useful for AI software and this consumes chip area and unnecessarily increases device costs when only AI operations are required. Commodity GPUs used in the home have started including specialist hardware to support "ray tracing" for example, which is a graphical operation that doesn't work well with vector processing. They have also started to include specialist regions for performing some AI workloads, acknowledging that the main vector processor is not the absolutely optimal approach. This leaves room in the market for pure AI devices that are hyper focussed on this application only and do not have all of the 3D graphics baggage attached.

One of the most well-known specialist AI devices is Google's TPU or "Tensor Processing Unit" which can offer a price/performance advantage over GPUs. More generally these devices are known as "systolic arrays" and other companies also produce them either for the open market or internal use only.

Conventional CPUs operate using "registers" which are small areas of very fast local memory that hold the intermediate results of calculations. A value is passed from a register to an Arithmetic and Logic Unit (ALU) which is a circuit for performing calculations. The result of the calculation is then stored back in a register. Then the next operation is performed which may mean passing the result stored in the register back to the same ALU again for another operation. A CPU can quickly run out of registers to hold intermediate calculation results and a value needed for a calculation might end up back in the main system RAM. Storing data here is dramatically slower than using a register and slows down the calculation significantly.

When performing matrix mathematics (which neural networks can be reduced to), the same calculation result is used over and over again. A systolic array has many ALUs (often several thousand) and these are directly connected together so a calculation result can flow straight from one ALU to another without any intermediate storage in a register which makes operations faster in this particular situation where calculation results are usually required to be involved in many more subsequent calculations. Opportunities for pipelining are also improved with this arrangement.

Systolic arrays expend considerably more of the limited available chip area on ALUs rather than using the chip area for registers, program control logic and other features typically found in a CPU. This means it has more of the chip area performing calculations in parallel at any one time than a CPU can achieve. The systolic array though is only of any use in special situations such as matrix arithmetic and is hopeless as a general purpose CPU.

Wafer Scale Integration

Silicon chips are currently most commonly produced on 12" diameter silicon wafers. The wafer is diced into smaller segments and each segment becomes an individual chip. The maximum practical size of an individual chip is dictated by the rate of faults experienced in manufacturing.

As larger chips are produced, there is a greater probability of any one chip on the wafer containing a flaw. It only takes a speck of dust to land on a chip during manufacturing and it develops a fault. If an attempt is made to produce chips that are too large, most of the chips on a wafer will have faults. There is therefore a maximum economic size to a chip described by the probability of manufacturing faults occurring. This limits how many transistors may be placed on one chip and consequently how much processing one single chip can do.

Many chips can be linked together, but much of the cost of a chip is around the packaging and installation on a circuit board. Additionally, connecting two chips together via a circuit board reduces performance versus communicating within the chip itself as the wire length is much longer. It also increases the power consumption which subsequently causes design difficulties getting rid of the heat produced. Wafer scale integration is the idea of using the entire silicon wafer as if it were one giant chip and not splitting it into smaller chips. The intent is to avoid these costs and problems.

The difficulty is that some proportion of every single wafer produced will not work and the section that is faulty will be entirely random and cannot be predicted at the time the chip is designed. It is not possible to produce a single wafer that is fully functional (without extreme luck). Wafer scale integration devices are specifically designed to assume some of the wafer will be faulty and electrically route around glitches when the device is tested. The idea has been around since the 1970s but in more recent times some companies have got it to work and wafer scale devices are now being routinely used for AI training tasks.

Leasing Compute Capability

The training phase to produce a model is very computationally intensive but it may be the case that the inference costs are much lower. It is often the case that the costs are the other way around, if for example a company has a hugely successful mass-market AI product with millions of users, the inference costs might end up being vastly larger than the training cost. However, for a lesser used model, perhaps an internal business application or a niche product, the training costs may take the lion's share of the budget and inference requires hardly any computation at all.

In this situation where a large amount compute is required but only for a short period, it may make economic sense to lease the compute required for training. Vast AI training compute is now widely available to anyone at many cloud providers with just a credit card needed to access it. Essentially any number of GPUs can be rented by the minute at a moment's notice.

Usually the providers are able to offer rental of GPU types that might be otherwise unaffordable to a small organisation such as GPUs with exceptionally large memories. Some providers also offer access to specialist training hardware that might be otherwise unaffordable or unavailable on the open market.

Peer to Peer Approaches

Some types of AI training task can be split over many machines. A large business may already have hundreds or even thousands of relatively powerful multi-core desktop PCs that sit idle 16 hours a day on weekdays and are idle 24 hours a day on weekends, when not in use by office workers. The machines may often be left powered on in order to receive software updates. This computational power can equate to a free supercomputer and potentially be harnessed to perform distributed training with appropriate business buy-in.

If the application is a common good cause e.g. medical research or the production of an open source product, thousands of willing volunteers may be found on the internet with very powerful machines they may be willing to donate to a training task. Many such distributed computing projects have successfully operated for decades performing other types of computation for the public good. If the cause is inspiring, usually people can be found who would like to help.

Neuromorphic Devices

GPUs, systolic arrays and wafer scale chips are commercially available products that have been in use for some time. There are some more exotic forms of neural network devices that exist mainly in research labs although there are a small number of commercially available examples.

Neuromorphic devices typically attempt to mimic the operation of a biological neuron in hardware as opposed to numerically simulating it mathematically as most current approaches do. Each neuron is a real physical thing in this approach and not just a simulation composed of a bunch of numbers in a matrix. This may be achieved by exploiting the physical properties of some, usually electrical, device in such a way as it mimics the operation of a neuron. The approaches used may involve analogue electronics rather than digital or use specialist memory technologies less commonly encountered in conventional computation.

Optical Devices

It is possible to perform AI computations using optics instead of electrical circuits and optical devices are now becoming practical. Light can travel through silicon and existing processes used to manufacture conventional electrical chips can be repurposed to produce optical devices. A waveguide splits laser light into two phases and computation is performed via either constructive or destructive interference between the two phases. The advantage is potentially considerably higher speeds than electrical devices with very low power consumption.

Quantum Supremacy

Quantum computers used to be science fiction but are now very much a real product that can be purchased by a well-funded organisation. Setting the weights on a neural network is essentially a search problem. A quantum computer has the potential to be able to try large ranges of the possibilities all at once using a brute force approach and may be able to train a neural network with the perfect weights in an instant, rather than the procedure taking days, weeks or months as currently. Well perhaps not instantly for a practical implementation but the thought is a quantum machine should theoretically be able to outpace conventional computing (or classical computing as it is known) by a very wide margin. The machine learning technique that best maps to a quantum computer may not be a neural network either but something else.

The main issue with quantum computers is scale. The current generation quantum machines cannot operate on very large problems. There is a grandiose term of "quantum supremacy" that sounds like something found in the pages of a thriller novel, but all it means is the point at which use of a quantum computer becomes economic over conventional computing approaches. Quantum supremacy is variously claimed by researchers, but the term is context dependent on the specific application for which quantum supremacy has been achieved. At the time of writing no quantum machine exists that can do neural network training in a way that rivals a cluster of GPUs on an economic basis. It is possible though that future quantum machines may be the ultimate method of training very large machine learning systems.

Quantum machines of the future may be capable of training vastly larger neural networks than are currently feasible and also arrive at the best possible training solution rather than a "close enough" approximation as in current training approaches. It's definitely worth keeping an eye on developments in the technology but it is not currently a practical approach.

Embedded AI

There is another end to the AI market where specialist hardware is used and that is in embedded devices. These are products often described as "internet of things" devices such as security cameras, voice assistants and home sensors. The problem with these devices is not achieving the highest levels of performance but achieving very low cost and sometimes very low power consumption to work within the constraints of batteries. A conventional CPU might be able to trivially tackle these small-scale applications but winds up being too expensive or results in excessive power consumption. Small AI accelerators can be built into cost-sensitive devices to enable a cheaper and lower power CPU to be used. The AI accelerator might be on the same chip as the CPU to lower the cost of the silicon.

Sometimes the aim is to take some of the workload away from a central data centre. This is known as "edge computing". A current generation voice assistant might be comprised of little more than an internet connected microphone and speaker, essentially it is just a telephone connecting through to a central service. All of the AI processing is actually performed at a remote data centre (in "the cloud"). These cloud resources cost money every time the device is used. A manufacturer might prefer to offload some of the computational cost to the device itself and have the customer purchase some of the required computing resource to reduce the cloud expenses. Perhaps part of the speech recognition is performed on the device for example.

A security camera might be tasked with determining if it can see a person. Part of the job might be done on the camera and then it sends the image to the cloud only if it believes a person could be present. Much more sophisticated software at the data centre double checks the image. This therefore avoids the data centre needing to continuously review the entire video feed, which is very expensive. The simplistic AI software on the camera might be set-up to err on the side of caution (be more prone to generate false positives) to ensure that detection does not fail, but the total amount of work performed with the complex software at the expensive data centre will be much less.

Embedded AI is also of interest to more expensive devices such as mobile phones and tablets. These are increasingly offering AI features, such as image and video manipulation. The manufacturer might prefer this is performed at least partially on the device to reduce the remote processing costs.

Very Large Models

The latest and greatest AI models are very large indeed and it is difficult to fit the entire model in the memory of a typical server. Even more problematically, training and inference is more often than not performed on GPUs because they are faster than a CPU at these tasks. GPUs routinely use specialist memory local to the card which is even smaller than that of a server and not usually easily upgradeable either. The GPU can access the main server memory, but doing so causes the GPU to lose much of its performance advantage over a CPU. The amount of memory available to a high end GPU is suitable for a large number of machine learning tasks and may never trouble the average AI developer, but for the most advanced leading edge models, memory limitations present a barrier to progress. This leads to the question as to whether many GPUs can be used in parallel.

If the model is smaller than the amount of memory on a video card, multiple GPUs can be easily used concurrently to perform inference, we just copy the same model onto multiple cards and farm out queries to all of the cards in parallel. There are also widely used methods for using multiple GPUs for training by doing machine learning on the same model on many cards and sharing the intermediate training progress. This again relies on the model size not exceeding the amount of memory on any single video card in the cluster.

It is possible in some circumstances to get a model trained for a large memory card to run inference on a smaller card for which it was not designed. Neural networks can often be easily split into multiple parts (e.g. across layer boundaries). The first part of the model can be run, the results saved, then another part of the model swapped in from SSD (replacing the first part of the model in memory). Swapping in a model segment into the GPU takes a couple of seconds but if there are not too many swaps, using the video card even with the swapping penalty can still exceed the performance of using a multi-core CPU. It's a considerably slower method than using a GPU with the appropriate amount of RAM though.

Time can be saved if many jobs can be run as a batch. Several jobs can be run on the first part of the model all at once, then the batches completed on the second part of the model after the model swap. So there is only one model swap penalty for many inference jobs. If the number of jobs in the batch is very large and the results are not needed immediately, the swap penalty can be successfully amortised.

This technique though is of no use if the results are needed quickly e.g. if the model is being used for an interactive application.

If multiple video cards are available but no single card is of sufficient size to hold the model it is possible to chain the cards together. For example a model may be split in two, the first part hosted on one card and the second part on another. The CPU reads out the hidden layer output from the first card, passing it to the next hidden layer input hosted on the second card to work against. When the second card has started running the second part of the job, it loads the first part of the next job onto the first card and starts running that in parallel. This is essentially a technique called pipelining that is often used in electronics.

Due to the ability of neural networks to be split across a boundary, it is also possible to do training of a large model on multiple cards. Part of the model may be hosted on one card and part on another. The back-propagation from one card can be transferred into the other card at the boundary of the model split. This does present some computational efficiency challenges leaving one card or other idle for some period of time leading to under-utilisation. In other words, two video cards are not twice as fast at model training as one due to efficiency losses. A single monolithic card with the relevant memory size and performance would be quicker if it is available.

There are some convoluted techniques to try and deal with efficiency loss and make sure that multiple cards stay loaded and don't idle waiting on results from other cards. While one card is idling it can partially start working on another data item (similar to the pipelining method). There are also techniques that rely on the organisation of specific classes of neural networks and the natural way in which they are partitioned internally which can be exploited to partition the neural network across multiple cards. This however very much depends on the application containing those natural boundary points.

Ensemble Learning

A different method of dealing with the problem that has received some attention is ensemble learning. The core idea is that several independent small models are used together. Each model in itself fits into the memory of a single video card and represents no issue to train. The models are used together as a collective to produce a better quality result than any single model can achieve on its own.

This is similar to how people organise expertise. One single person doesn't know everything. If you want medical expertise, you refer to a doctor. If you want to know about finance then you talk to your investment adviser. What is needed is an understanding of which expert to refer to in which situation and that is information that you have in your head. Even though you may know nothing at all about medicine yourself, you are capable of recognising what a medical issue looks like and which other specific human brain knows how to deal with it.

It might be possible to segment some machine learning problems across domains in exactly the same way. You might be able to find a really good cat detector and really good dog detector, then you just need an overarching model that can consider roughly if it thinks an image might be a cat or dog and refer to the appropriate expert.

It's also possible to segment a problem in more subtle ways. Part of the training examples for a single domain can be passed to a bunch of different models and then an aggregator can be added. Say for example the problem is recognising aircraft. Part of the training examples can be passed to one model and part to another. One model might get mostly Boeing aircraft and another model might end up with Airbus examples. An overarching model might then learn from test data which model is generally better at which kind of example. If it thinks it could be looking at a Boeing it might lean more towards the advice of that expert model but still somewhat accept the opinion from the Airbus model.

The overarching model is somewhat like the chair of a board meeting, behaving as a generalist but learning which deep expert to take advice from in each specific situation. Rather than specifically learning how to refer to one expert in their entirety, the chair learns how to blend information, perhaps taking 80% of the advice from one person and 20% of the advice from another. The trick is working out how much to listen to each expert in the context of each situation.

Ensembles can also work in a pipeline arrangement as well. The first model produces an estimate as to the answer and then passes that to a second model that learns the errors that the first model commonly makes. Therefore it refines and corrects what the first model doesn't know. This arrangement can be known as "boosting" ensembles.

LoRA

LoRA stands for "Low Rank Adaptive fine tuning". This is a training technique for adapting an existing model to a specific task. An existing very large model that was expensive to train and requires a lot of hardware, such as an LLM, can be specialised giving it new capabilities. For example an LLM that knows nothing about car maintenance can be given new training data and acquire expertise in this new subject. This still involves training the entire model though. The length of training may be much shorter but it requires a lot of hardware.

The LoRA method evaluates which specific parts of a large model need to be updated. Perhaps as little as 1% of the original model may need to be modified. Consequently it requires considerably less hardware to perform a LoRA adaptation than to train a model as a whole.

An interesting property of LoRAs is that the adaptations can be swapped in and out dynamically. For example a model can be suddenly made an expert on a particular subject and then that expertise removed and replaced with some different expertise. This ability to rapidly swap capabilities can be used as a form of ensemble learning. If it can first be detected which kind of expertise is needed, perhaps using a classifier, then the appropriate LoRA can be swapped in on demand.

LoRAs can work on many kinds of models. Many LoRAs exist for image generation models as well as text. Early image generation models were notoriously bad at producing realistic images of hands when generating people. LoRAs are one method of fixing this issue. A specialised hand generator can be swapped in when a person is being produced.

Model Simplification

Neural networks typically work with floating point numbers. Originally 32-bit floating point numbers were used (occupying 4 bytes of memory each) almost exclusively as a common level of precision that was widely available on most GPU hardware. However, it has been discovered that many large models can work quite effectively at much lower numerical precision. Consequently many current generation GPUs have a 16-bit precision mode. This means that a model of twice the size can be fitted into the same memory as a 32-

bit model as a 16-bit number only occupies 2 bytes of memory. The reduced precision often has very little noticeable impact on the performance of the model

It's been found that many large language models can still work effectively at extraordinarily low precision, as little as 4-bit or even 2-bit precision. Moving to this level is known as model "quantisation" and enables a large computational performance boost if the output of the model is found to be sufficient at these levels.

There are also model "compression" techniques. These attempt to work out which regions of a model have the least influence on the output and remove them, therefore reducing the size of the model. Model compression is useful for producing minimised versions of models to run on less capable hardware such as mobile phones. The compressed model isn't quite as good as the uncompressed version, but delivers most of the benefit in a smaller footprint.

The Future

No one can predict the future, least of all AI book authors, but extrapolations can be attempted as to where the technology could be going. There is currently an unprecedented amount of investment being poured into AI. Hundreds of new companies are forming, existing technology companies are quickly pivoting their focus and many interesting new developments emerging at a substantial rate of pace. Some of these directions might be fruitful, some might be less productive but there are certainly interesting times ahead.

At the time of writing generative AI is currently on an upward trend in the hype cycle, not having yet reached the peak of inflated expectations. As is always the case in such a cycle, there will be an inevitable decline in popularity as the boundaries and limitations become apparent but generative technology is now firmly entrenched into daily life and is probably here to stay, at least within a number of prominent niches. In only a few short months the technology has come to be widely used for general question answering and may challenge the dominance of conventional web search engines. The major search engine companies seem to be sufficiently concerned as to be making vast investments of billions of dollars into the technology just in case it should displace their very lucrative business models. They are probably right to be worried as the generative systems could well absorb at least a noticeable part of their business in short order and become the new first choice method for finding information. Why would you want to click through a bunch of links when you can just have a machine directly give you the answer you need first time? It seems entirely realistic that method of interacting with search could become preferred.

Generative AI has been found to be very useful for software development and is likely to remain in that market in some form. It is effective at synthesising short code snippets and is a helpful code search engine for assisting programmers. Claims that it may displace developers entirely are likely overblown, previous such technologies did not and the number of developers has risen if anything. However, LLMs are a demonstrably useful tool for software development that will likely help accelerate the process of coding.

Creative writing may similarly see some change. It is unlikely that LLM models can displace fiction authors on any near timeframe, but the products can make helpful suggestions and enhance the creative process. The tools can come up with ideas for how a story might progress and write sample paragraphs. The author of the future might become more of an editor, approving and rewriting paragraphs initially constructed by an LLM and weaving them together into a narrative.

The process of writing a work of fiction may become much quicker than it used to be. It has always been the case that some authors have used ghostwriters to fill in boilerplate in their own style to enable them to churn out their novels faster. The LLM might be in effect replacing the job of ghostwriter more than it is replacing the primary author. The author of the future might roughly outline what they want to happen in a story and an LLM can produce some sample prose along those lines. If nothing else an LLM can likely assist less capable authors with the quality of the prose, perform grammar checking and provide suggestions for rephrasing to a much more sophisticated degree than current generation software.

The stock photographer is one career that may now have fallen at the hands of AI. Models have already become quite effective at producing this style of image. The quality of photos generated has some rough edges but it seems like the final brick will be placed in the wall and these issues will be ironed out. It is quite possible to now ask for a photograph of two people pointing at a computer and have one produced in seconds. No need to pay for a photographer or indeed hire any actors to appear in the images. When free is competing with relatively expensive, a few rough edges will probably go unnoticed.

Cartoonist might be a career that is AI enabled in the future. The job of producing the artwork can be outsourced to generative systems. The job of cartoonist will probably not disappear, someone still needs to come up with the situation described in the comic strip and write the comedy. Someone is needed to arrange the characters and show how they will react to each other. The actual production of the final drawing though may be outsourced to a machine and become deskilled. This could mean that a lot more comics are produced.

More generally AI systems can now replace some functions of an artist. Image to image systems can enable someone unskilled to draw a rough outline of what they would like to see and the system can convert it into a photorealistic image. Generative systems can create a photograph from an idea and then style transfer can emulate the appearance of any artistic style.

The fashion model may be on the way out as systems exist that can produce highly realistic video of a person walking and AI can realistically overlay the couture of a particular designer. The future fashion model may be the customer as the systems can equally transfer the clothing onto a constructed video of the potential purchaser to show how they may look as opposed to the clothing being shown on someone else. Several mobile apps have attempted to do this.

Machine learning driven speech synthesisers are now very good and are on the edge of becoming indistinguishable from real people. Voice artists could be in jeopardy in the future, at least for mundane work. It seems likely that real human voice artists will still be preferred for movies as the value is as much in the name of the artist as a marketing brand as it is in the voice work itself. However, in lower value productions, such as reading out an audio book, podcasts, online videos, corporate training and advertising it would seem that automated systems will prevail. The systems are not quite there yet and require some direction with respect to prosody, tone and emotion to avoid a flat reading, but are improving.

Another possible consequence of machine learning driven speech is for music in that backing vocalists may be out of luck. Speech synthesisers can be trained to sing as easily as they can be trained to speak. This might result in backing tracks being sung by AI or other parts of the song that do not feature the principal artist. It seems unlikely that the artist singing lead vocals in music intended for entertainment would often be automated, however music for corporate purposes may be sung entirely by machine e.g. in adverts where the brand of the artist is not as relevant as the music itself. A hobbyist production might also make use of an AI lead vocalist where the musician cannot afford to employ human talent for a work that may not generate much or any revenue.

As well as generating novel voices, AI speech synthesis can simulate the voice of any real person. This might cause the extension of artists' careers who may have otherwise retired. Artists can now produce music in their later years with the same tone as when they were younger. Software has been used for many years for pitch correction but now the timbre of the voice can be corrected as well or the voice generated entirely from scratch. The same concept is already occurring with actors, some of whom have sold rights to use their distinctive voices after they have retired for use in future productions with which they will personally have little involvement.

Video can be manipulated with AI techniques. This technology has been used many times in movies for face replacement, particularly for effects such as replacing older actors with their younger selves for flash-back scenes and overlaying stunt actor performances with the appearance of the main actor. With an AI face and an AI voice, the actor is perhaps no longer necessary at all though. This might mean particularly popular actors may appear in multiple productions at the same time. The demand for actors might generally reduce with a decreasing selection of particularly popular actors appearing in more movies.

An interesting use of video manipulation has been in foreign language dubbing. An English speaking actor can now become fluent in Chinese, or in fact any other language as the video is modified to adjust the lip sync to be in line with the actor that is dubbing them (or in fact it is possible to produce a version of their own voice speaking the other language). Audiences can now enjoy foreign films as if they were produced directly for the home audience without the inconvenience of out-of-sync speech. The same technology is also being made more widely available. It may be possible to have a machine translated video call with someone in a foreign language that you do not speak with an AI driven rendition of your own voice speaking the other language with correct lip sync, albeit with perhaps a few seconds of latency while the system has a chance to work out what you are saying.

As with the fashion model, the background artist (or "extra") in a movie or TV show may no longer be required when the actors can simply be generated with any appropriate appearance. The main cast of the production might be real actors, but any character that is only minor or incidental to the plot may be generative AI. Producing precisely directable movie quality characters is beyond the capability of current generative video techniques, but possibly not for too much longer.

Computer generated backgrounds have been used for some time in TV shows. The actors are actually performing against a green screen (or wall-sized LED display) and only a small portion of the set may physically exist, or in some cases nothing at all. Creating sets is expensive but even easily available filming locations can prove costly. The location may need to be rented, a street closed down, traffic management paid for, bureaucratic permissions acquired and security posted. It's considerably cheaper to simulate a location with a green screen where possible. Building a convincing high quality computer generated 3D model of a set that can change perspective with the camera movements is also not cheap, but with new generative techniques, this may be a cost that comes down. Building complex sets and filming at famous locations may become within the budget of the small-scale movie producer. AI techniques may also be able to resolve problems such as applying the correct lighting to the actors to match the simulated background such that they blend in convincingly with what is depicted on the green screen.

Generative AI can be used to generate music from scratch. At the time of writing this hasn't taken off commercially to the same degree as with image and text generation but it is quite effective nonetheless. Generative AI for music is available in research with reasonably high quality results. Music can be created from a text prompt in much the same way as an image can. The style of music required can be described in detail and the system will generate something novel based on that description. The style of music produced can also be conditioned by providing an existing song, in other words it is possible to generate new music in the style of an existing artist. The music artist is unlikely to disappear but as with the stock photographer, jobs producing generic background music to accompany TV and online videos could be in jeopardy.

Current generation high-end AI acceleration hardware is almost fast enough to generate new unique audio in real time. In a few more hardware generations real time music generation may be feasible on inexpensive machines. Instead of choosing a streaming playlist or radio station with your favourite genre, you may simply describe what kind of music you like in words, perhaps with a speech interface. Your phone or other audio device will simply produce infinite new unique music in that genre on demand. Alternatively you may supply a set of existing songs and ask for something new that sounds somewhat like what you have.

Curiously, entirely computer generated music bands have also been tried several times with the artists being entirely fictional characters generated by machine to the specification of the music company. Whether this idea will stick or not remains to be seen. It seems intuitively likely that people will be more interested in human artists that really exist and will be less inclined to follow fictional artists but perhaps there will be some niches. There have been some examples in the past of fictional characters having significant musical success. As far back as 1966 "The Monkees" were a fictional band that originated from a TV show and became successful in the real world. The 1998 founded Gorillaz band consists of animated fictional characters and has been very successful. Perhaps computer generated characters are the modern incarnation of this idea. Fictional bands haven't previously been a widely embraced phenomenon but more of an occasional novelty, with the vast majority of artists being real people. If the idea does take off to any degree, AI is ready to serve.

Conversational AIs may start appearing in household products and they might be voice activated and start understanding the user's intentions to a more sophisticated extent.[4] It might be possible to shout vague instructions at a television and have it understand what you mean. Perhaps you might order "play that old movie with the dinosaurs that escape" rather than recalling the name of the film and trying to find wherever it may be on the user interface using a remote control. An LLM can be prompted to understand that it is likely dealing with requests for television content and decode whatever attempt the user makes at describing what they want. An appropriately prompted current generation LLM easily gets "Jurassic Park" as the correct answer to that question (exactly as previously phrased) with no problem even though the name of the movie was never mentioned.

A conversational AI can also make suggestions as to content the user may wish to watch and the user can refine the LLMs suggestions. The user might say "I want to watch a movie something like Star Wars" and the LLM can suggest

---

4   Would you like any toast?

appropriate films. Trying this with a current generation LLM suggests:

- Any of the Star Trek franchise
- Guardians of the Galaxy
- The Fifth Element
- Dune
- Ender's Game

These may not be the perfect suggestions but they are all science fiction movies involving space themes that could possibly entertain someone who enjoyed Star Wars.

Televisions might incorporate AI that can look at the content of the image as well. For example, the television may be requested to notify a football fan if a goal is scored and only then play the video. This service currently exists but is dependent on having a real person watch the game and marking the appropriate moments, hence it's only available for some sport. A future TV might be able to respond to these kinds of requests without the aid of a human operator and work against any content regardless of how obscure.

A future TV may also be able to edit down any game to a user's requested length. A 90 minute recorded football match could be edited to 10 minutes of highlights with an AI selecting the most pivotal moments. Possibly a movie director's sleep-inducing four hour magnum opus might be automatically edited down into a more exciting and pacy 60 minutes of viewing leaving the full length spectacle for the real fans. Or given the high quality of LLM summarisations, it could provide you with a short recap explaining what happened after you dozed off.

Future linear TV may also be moderately personalised. It is already commonplace for movies to be slightly edited based on country, to insert a cameo appearance by a particularly popular local actor for example. A TV could also edit a movie to show you your preferred version by making minor adjustments. For example if you are bored by an extended fight scene and prefer to see more of the back-story and world building it could produce your preferred edit. Someone else's preferences may be entirely the other way around. A movie producer might release everything they have on the cutting room floor and the system can edit together the user's perfect version on-demand.

AI techniques will probably be the next deployment in the cat and mouse game between advertisers and those who are less keen on viewing the ads. AI can quite easily detect advertising breaks in programming and edit them out. However, it is also useful on the other side of the fence. AI has for many years been widely deployed in systems to decide which web adverts will be displayed to users based on their demographics and recent viewing history. Use in this field will presumably only expand. Other techniques such as image generation and in-painting can potentially seamlessly weave product placements into TV programmes that are specific to each viewer. The canned drink the soap-opera star is holding may now be your personal favourite brand of beer, flawlessly edited in dynamically by your own TV. The advertising boards surrounding a sports stadium may show adverts specific to each viewer personally as the computing power in a television becomes sufficient to perform the AI replacement tricks in real time. While viewers may have limited interest in such technology, advertisers probably will.

Conversational AIs might be able to bring computer games to life as never before. Role playing games are currently very popular but the characters have never been terribly conversant. This is likely to change quite soon as they are connected up to LLMs, which are now capable of following a script and playing a particular character role quite effectively. That orc or elf in the game can now have a complete conversation with you whilst in character and understand requests to complete tasks. Using LoRA style techniques the output can be modified to be in a particular writing style consistent with the game. The generation can be pre-seeded with prompting describing the role the character is supposed to be playing. Using retrieval augmented generation, the character can refer to facts outside of the scope of the prompting. A game designer may provide a book-length novel describing the world and the character can pick up lore from the text.

Since the game "Elite" was released on the BBC Micro in 1984, simplistic forms of generative techniques have been used to provide the impression of vast gaming universes to explore that have not been directly programmed but created by the machine dynamically in real time. Modern generative techniques might be able to expand gaming world boundaries to provide limitless universes created to the broad design of the game author that would be far too time consuming to program by hand.

AI tools have become available that can produce 3D objects, which is currently a very expensive process requiring skilled artists. An artist may work for days on constructing a 3D model of a car. In the future, a game developer may simply show an AI an example photo of a car and ask for a model to be produced that is similar. AI tools can even work out what an object might look like from the other side and do not require photographs from all angles. Tools can "rig" objects, that is work out how they should move and deform e.g. the doors of a car should open and the wheels should turn. AI is also capable of defining realistic motion for an object. This might dramatically reduce the production costs of games and lower the barrier to entry, resulting in more games that can achieve higher standards of graphical quality without requiring vast budgets.

For some time now AI upscaling has been applied to games (known as Deep Learning Super Sampling) such that lower quality graphics can be rendered at a higher resolution. For example, the resolution or frame rate of a game may be doubled. In the future such techniques may be taken to greater extremes with comparatively crude graphics being input as a placeholder to show the rough layout of a scene and enhanced in real time using AI techniques to photorealistic quality. This may mean complex 3D models are not needed.

In the physical world, AI robots will likely be taking over more jobs. Self driving taxi services are now operating in some regions. Self driving trucks are entirely possible. If these services become mainstream they may cause significant disruption to the transport market. The equipment is currently very expensive, the finances of the self-driving vehicle companies are opaque and it may not be genuinely competitive with a human driver at the moment without the subsidies of big tech companies. However, automation will become cheaper with economies of scale once the technology is worked out and may start to undercut human drivers on price.

It is often tempting to exaggerate the extent and speed to which changes to the job market might take place, the real pace of change may be quite slow, but change is coming. Transport companies have a significant investment in manually driven vehicles which may be expected to last twenty years or more. It might not make any economic sense to replace an expensive newly purchased manually driven truck or taxi with an automated version until it reaches end of life. Even though a human driver might be more expensive, the sunk cost of the vehicle keeps people employed at least for a while. There are likely some situations where a self-driving vehicle is not safe. They are often tested on wide, car friendly streets with easy driving in perpetually sunny climes. The vehicles might not cope well in poor visibility on a snowy mountain pass, which keeps humans employed to do the difficult parts of the job.

Problems can arise, progress is slow and the technology may have its ups and down, but the general direction is probably near full automation in transport. As well as the negative problems of job losses, there will be benefits. Self driving cars will on average make fewer mistakes leading to lives saved on the roads. More people can have access to transport, such as the young, the elderly and the disabled who may be currently without an effective transport solution due to inability to drive a vehicle or the unwillingness of insurance companies to cover them.

People can be concerned that self-driving vehicles may increase car use and jam up the roads. In urban centres where traffic density is a problem, self-driving technology can also be applied to public transport with improvements in convenience. A future urban bus service may be self-driving and operate more like a large taxi seating a dozen or more people. The bus can be called on demand as opposed to arriving on a fixed schedule. In dense urban environments, multiple passengers will probably be found roughly along the same route at the same time and a bus can stop to pick up several customers. Appropriate buses can also be called to suit passenger requirements, such as a bus with wheelchair space and a ramp, or a bus with extra storage for large bags. Those with mobility problems might apply for a special exemption to have a bus call directly at their home as opposed to at a bus stop somewhere down the street.

In the logistics industry generally, there are fewer and fewer jobs that cannot be automated by AI driven robots. Fully automated cranes can now load cargo ships with containers, which may be arriving on automated trucks. It is possible to sail a cargo ship with full automation and then unload it with another automated crane. When the truck arrives at a warehouse, people are most usually involved with unloading the container contents, but that job too can be automated. In many large warehouses, robots are now routinely moving products around and retrieving them from the shelves. Robots are at least partially, and in a few cases entirely, involved in packing customer orders.

Small robots are being trialled in some places for final mile delivery of products to a customer's home. These robots are in effect a mobile locker service. They often travel at low speed on pavements and contact a customer via mobile app when they arrive at the delivery address. The customer must then go outside and enter a code to unlock the robot and retrieve the order.

AI driven systems are being increasingly used in agriculture to perform repetitive work such as picking crops and weeding. The systems use cameras to identify ripe fruit and learn how to correctly grasp it without causing damage, or they identify weeds and can then use a laser to destroy it. These systems may end up replacing a great deal of seasonal labour.

Machine learning systems may be coming to assist in more skilled occupations too such as medicine. It may be the case in the future that AI is involved in a majority of medical diagnoses. AI may interpret the results of scans to determine what could be wrong with the patient using a vast database of knowledge. There have been a number of attempts at this already with varying degrees of success. In the short term, AI may be able to help to the greatest degree in the field of radiology as classification of images is now very robust. AI systems may soon be as good as any doctor at examining an X-ray or MRI scan.

Future legal work may involve more AI. Systems can check complex contracts and confirm that standard clauses have not been missed. AI systems can assess the merits of a claim and use all available legal precedents to advise if legal action is likely to be successful, potentially saving a client a lot of money. Systems can perform legal checks in house conveyancing and advise regarding any anomalies.

In education AI systems may be able to act as a teaching assistant. It is possible to persuade an LLM to behave somewhat as a teacher, guiding a student step-by-step through a process of learning about a particular topic and adapting to what the student enters. For example the student may have been set a task to write an essay about a work of Shakespeare. The student writes only a couple of sentences, which may be about any of the plays. The LLM can then suggest how to expand the essay by referring to elements of the plays but without actually doing the work of the student for them.

AI may prove a boon for people with disabilities. Any reasonably clear audio source can now be real-time captioned to a fair standard to assist the hard of hearing. This software may begin to achieve better performance with worse quality audio and start to interpret contextual hints from associated video to choose the right words with greater success. It is also possible speech recognition may be able to caption people speaking in real time and present a transcription on AR glasses. An array microphone with a camera system may also be able to accurately position one person in a noisy room and pick out the audio from whoever you are currently looking at to clarify it, resolving a problem with current generation hearing aids.

For those with vision problems, high quality human-level speech synthesis can convert any text into much more listenable and less fatiguing audio than the robotic sounding voices of the past. Any book can now be an audiobook. Image captioning generative systems can describe what is contained in a photograph rather than relying on a book publisher or web page author to have taken the time to caption it. Any TV programme could potentially be automatically audio described in the same way as opposed to just some programs. Systems may be able to describe the view from a camera with greater finesse and guide people to objects.

Demand for AI is increasing in consumer products and the electronics market is adapting to serve that need. Consumer devices are now beginning to include AI processors as standard that can accelerate the execution of AI inference tasks directly on the devices. These chips are currently performing functions such as resolution scaling to enhance the apparent fidelity of video, speech recognition and photo manipulation. AI processing chips will likely increase in sophistication and performance as time goes on. As the memory available to mobile devices improves, these chips might become good enough to execute viable large language models locally without requiring the backing of a data centre.

AI is likely to become ever more strongly woven into the fabric of society. The true power lies in the ability to augment human potential, catalysing innovation and propelling us into a more promising future. Some challenges await but AI is poised to revolutionise industries, enhance productivity and streamline business processes on an unprecedented scale. As we continue to harness these capabilities, AI will not only reshape the way we work, communicate, and live but also create a new world of exciting possibilities.

Index

OP

Hey Chatbot, can you write me a
book about AI please?

No.

www.ingramcontent.com/pod-product-compliance
Lightning Source LLC
LaVergne TN
LVHW051435050326
832903LV00030BD/3098